COMPLETE beauty BOOK

HELEN FOSTER

p

This is a Parragon Book
This edition published in 2003

Parragon
Queen Street House
4 Queen Street
Bath BA1 1HE, UK

Copyright © Parragon 2002

Paperback ISBN: 1-40541-741-2

Hardback ISBN: 1-40541-642-4

A copy of the CIP data for this book is available from
the British Library upon request.

The rights of Helen Foster to be identified as the
author of this work have been asserted in accordance
with Section 77 of the Copyright, Designs and Patents
Act of 1988.

The author and the publishers of the book have made every effort to ensure that the
information contained in this book is accurate and as up-to-date as possible at the date of
publication. It is advised that this book should not be used as an alternative to seeking specialist
advice (especially with regard to queries on health issues). Any reliance upon the accuracy of the
information contained in this book is entirely at the reader's own risk.

All information contained in this book is provided without responsibility on part of the author
and publishers and to the full extent permissible by law. The author and publishers accept no
liability for any loss or damage (whether direct, indirect, consequential or otherwise) or injury
arising as a result of any reliance (whether express or implied) on the advice or information set
out in the book.

Any information or advice given in this book is meant for guidance purpose only and readers are
responsible for determining whether such information or advice applies to their particular
situation. The information and advice should not be relied upon as statements or representation
of facts. No warranty is given as to the accuracy of any information given.

WARNING At all times, readers should ensure that they read and follow any safety
instructions contained in the book.

Printed in Indonesia

contents

introduction

How do you feel when you look in the mirror each morning? Do you like what you see?

Would you prefer your eyes to be wider, your skin to be softer, your hair to be fuller? If you would you're the average woman – there are very few women alive who are happy with their looks. It's reported that Naomi Campbell hates her feet and that Catherine Zeta Jones thinks her eyes are too small. These are two of the most beautiful women in the world – if they're not happy, what hope do the rest of us have? Well there is loads of hope. You see, the marvellous thing about beauty is that no matter how you look naturally – how puffy-eyed, spotty-skinned or limp-haired – with the right equipment and the right techniques you can improve yourself. And with that improvement comes increased self-confidence and self-love – two of the most beautiful (and of course important) qualities any woman can possess.

Now, the problem with all this is that the beauty industry is rife with nonsense that plays on our need to feel good about ourselves. There are soaps that claim to melt fat, pills that say they'll remove wrinkles and herbal products that promise to do everything from curing baldness to boosting your bust size. In 99.9 per cent of cases, the claims are complete rubbish. Which is where we come in. This book breaks through the hype and the puff. It's going to go back to basics, giving you the products, techniques and tips you need to maximize your assets. By the end of it you'll be armed with all the information you need to make the most of yourself inside and out: to emphasize the points you love and disguise the bits you loathe – and just to feel happy with yourself. Are you ready? Then let's begin.

which colour suits you?

Stand in front of any beauty counter and you'll see there are hundreds of eye, lip and nail colours to choose from. Which you pick can make a massive difference – a shade that's wrong for you can make you look pale and washed out; on mature skins it can highlight wrinkles and age you by 10 years. Knowing how to choose the right hues for you is vital to helping yourself look your best.

The good news is you can wear pretty much any colour you want, so long as you pick the right shade. To do this you need to know two things. The first is your hair colour (the one you have now rather than the one you were born with). This shows you the depth or brightness of shade that will flatter you best – the lighter your hair, the lighter the shade that will suit you (and vice versa). The second is your skin tone. This helps reveal what shades of a colour will suit you best. To determine your skin tone, look at the inside of your wrist, while holding it over a piece of white paper. Is the skin a shade of white, pink, blue or grey (which means you have a cool skin tone and need cool shades); or yellow or brown (which means you have a warm skin tone and need warm shades)? To find your perfect colours, just look up your hair and skin tone combination in the pages that follow.

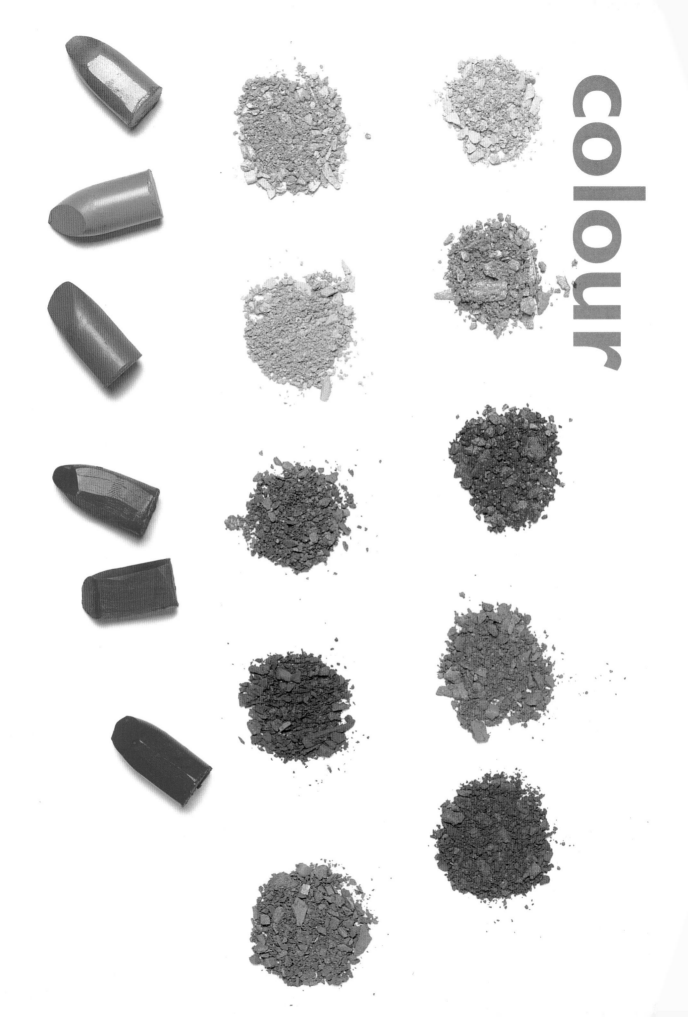

colour

blonde or
light brown hair
cool skin

Like:

Gwyneth Paltrow, Claudia Schiffer

Your best eye colours:

slate greys, sky or icy blues, lilacs and plums; navy

or grey mascara can also look better

than black

Your best blush:

sugary or rose pink

Your best lipsticks:

sugary pinks, lilacs, heathers or pinky browns

The worst thing any cool-skinned blonde can do is wear warm yellows and oranges. If you want to look ill, that's the way to do it. Instead you should base your look on cool, icy tones – particularly those with blue or pink undertones, as these are colours found in your skin and will therefore flatter you best. But be careful – too many light shades on your face in one go can make you look washed out. Ensure your look has a focus, be it a darker shadow or noticeable (not necessarily bright) lipstick. If you do want to wear pastel eyes and nude lips, apply lots of mascara. Finally, your big make-up mistake is wearing too much heavy blush: most blondes blush no darker than rosy pink, so going any deeper than this will look unnatural.

blonde or light brown hair warm skin

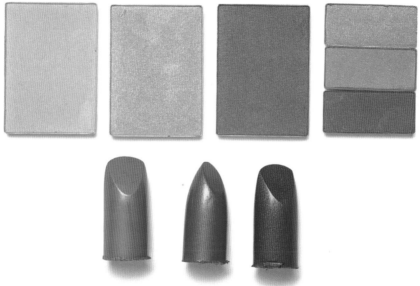

Like:

Jennifer Aniston, Geri Halliwell

Your best eye colours:

warm browns, shimmery golds and greens, pale yellows or peaches

Your best blush:

apricot or tawny brown

Your best lipsticks:

golden brown, corals, peachy pinks or bronzes

Your skin has gold or yellow undertones, so the most flattering colours for you contain these shades – bluey pinks or purples will make you look pale and washed out and will enhance any dark circles under your eyes. Lighter shades work best with your fairer hair and you should avoid any look that involves dark, heavy eyes and lips. You should also be careful with blush – if it's too heavy it will make your skin look paler and you older. To really light up your face, apply a little blush or bronzer to the apples of your cheeks and also the tip of your nose and chin, as this will enhance your warm colouring.

red hair
pale skin

Like:

Nicole Kidman, Julianne Moore

Your best eye colours:

peach, orange, khaki, light green and bronze

Your best blush:

if you must wear it, tawny pinks or light apricots

Your best lipsticks:

orangey reds, heathery pinks, terracotta browns, or apricots

The main rule with redheads and make-up is the simpler the better. Keep eyeshadows to one shade, define your brows (a must for many redheads) and tint your lips and you're ready to go. Green- or brown-based eye shades look great on you, but your skin tone can often be very pink, which means heathery pinks and plums will also suit you. Many redheads have high colour in their cheeks, so only use blush if you feel you really need it. Finally, if there's one shade every redhead should own it's a bright orangey red lipstick – with soft brown or green eyeshadow, it can look amazing. Like blondes, you should steer clear of black mascara, which looks unnatural. Choose brown instead, and never go without it – redheads' eyelashes are often very pale and need that hint of colour.

dark hair
pale skin

Like:

Anjelica Huston, Courteney Cox

Your best eye colours:

cool grey, black, ivory, silver and rich plum

Your best blush:

sugary or rose pink

Your best lipsticks:

fuchsia pinks, crimson reds, deep plums, or mauves

The strong contrast between your hair and skin means that dramatic make-up suits you best. If there's one colouring that can really carry off both dark eyes and strong lips it's yours. In fact, you break all the rules. While the shades in your skin tone (normally pinks, ivories and blues) will look good, contrast looks even better – particularly in the evening, when cool-toned, dark, smoky eyes (slate greys or bitter chocolate browns) and bright fuchsia or crimson lips will create the ultimate sophisticated look. Whatever you do, make sure you keep your blusher pale pink – sugary or rose tones are the most flattering. And don't forget lashes and brows – they are vital to frame striking looks.

dark hair warm skin

Like:

Jennifer Lopez, Cindy Crawford

Your best eye colours:

olive green, rust, beige, chocolate browns, earthy reds and oranges

Your best blush:

tawny browns or apricots – and a brightening pink for sleepy skin

Your best lipsticks:

rusts, raisins, warm chocolate brown or orangey reds

Nothing looks better on dark, olive colouring than deep shades of warm colours. Again, look hard at your skin and you'll see tones of olive green, ochre, russets, chocolate browns and earthy reds – which is why you should be choosing these in all your make-up. They'll just give your face a glow and a permanently sun-kissed look. For blush, tawny shades will suit you day to day, but buy a warm pink for when you feel tired. Fatigue can make olive skins look sallow; the pink counteracts this and brings your skin back to its normal shade. Pinks and blues are a no-no for you – as your skin is more yellow than caramel, they will make you look washed out.

light black skin dark hair

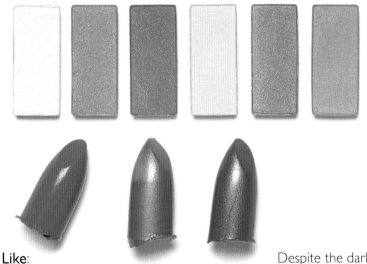

Like:

Halle Berry, Tyra Banks

Your best eye colours:

charcoal greys, bitter chocolate browns, pale pinks, lilacs and sky blues; mascara should be black or brown black

Your best blush:

shimmery pinks look great with pastel make-up, or try caramel shades if you're using dark make-up on your eyes

Your best lipsticks:

nude, bitter chocolate browns, pale shimmery pinks or warm browny pinks

Despite the darker pigmentation of your skin, you're often more cool-complexioned than warm. Many light black skins have an ashy tone, which means you'll see grey, beige and bone tints when you look at your wrist. Avoid the bright primary shades that are often recommended for black skin, as they'll overpower your creamy complexion, and go for intense pastel shades for dramatic contrast. Wear these with very natural lips to balance your face. If you don't want to use colour, dark eye and pale lip combinations look amazing on you. Some pale black skins do have warm tones. In this case, follow the advice on page 23 for colours, but use paler, pastel versions of them – and remember the less-is-more rule.

Dark black skin dark hair

Like:

Venus Williams, Alek Wek

Your best eye colours:

navy blues, deep plums, dark or reddish browns and golds

Your best blush:

plums or dark browns

Your best lipsticks:

raisin browns, deep or glossy plums, deep reds, chocolate browns

This can be the hardest colouring to find make-up for, as many companies don't understand dark skin. Aim for the deepest, warmest shade of any colour (particularly the reds, plums, blues and browns you find in your skin) and skip bright shades or anything with a cool blue or pink base. Shimmery shades look great – particularly in the evening – as do gloss lipsticks. For eyes choose the darkest, inkiest mascara to show your lashes off. Be careful when choosing foundation – many shades have ashy undertones, which can make you look washed out and ruin the effects of your carefully chosen make-up. Specialist ranges offer the best choice.

2

your skin

Beautiful skin is essential for making the most of your looks. Without it, all that carefully applied make-up will either go patchy and blotchy, slide into lines and wrinkles or disappear off your face in a shiny, oily mess. The simple truth is that most of us don't have beautiful skin. In fact, we don't even have so-called 'normal' skin, with its plump, shiny texture, radiant glow and minimal breakouts.

Instead we have dry bits, oily bits or irritated bits, and that means our skin doesn't always look or feel as good as it should. But the good news is that you don't have to put up with this. By knowing what kind of skin you have and how to treat it, you can solve your particular problems. Balance the levels of water and oil in your skin and you will create the state of harmony that is beautiful, perfect, 'normal' skin.

the skincare equipment kit

Creating perfect skin takes the right products – here's what you'll need.

Glycerine soaps and cleansing bars

Normal soap is too harsh for delicate facial skin, but bars that contain moisturizing ingredients are a great compromise for those who like the feel of soap and water.

Cream cleansers

Milky or creamy cleansers moisturize while they cleanse. For the best results apply them with your fingers, let them soak in and then remove them with cotton wool or tissues.

Foaming cleansers

For skins that need deeper cleansing or to remove thick sunscreens in summer, you can't beat foaming cleansers that you lather onto your skin and then rinse off with water.

Cleansing wipes

Wipes are perfect for women in a hurry or those who like low-maintenance skincare. Choose ones that are adapted for your skin type.

Make-up removers

Eye make-up needs special solvents to dissolve it fully, which makes a separate eye make-up remover essential.

Facial scrub

Gentle scrubs with microbeads or spheres of exfoliant will brighten up dull complexions.

Toners

The sophistication of skincare nowadays means that very few people need these, but if you want to use a toner choose one that's alcohol-free.

Glycerine bars in lemon, grapefruit, orange, lime and strawberry.

Light moisturizers

Gel- or lotion-based moisturizers are great for wearing during the day or for skin types that benefit from less oil and more water.

Heavy moisturizers

Thick, oil-based moisturizers are best for winter wear, or on very dry or ageing skin.

Clay face mask

Perfect for helping clear pores; mud masks have a similar effect.

Moisturizing face mask

Creamy masks give skin a moisture boost – good ingredients to look for are aqua, rosewater or seaweed.

Peel-off masks

Often based on cucumber, these masks exfoliate the skin and give the face a bright and healthy glow.

Eye creams

The skin around the eye is thinner and more sensitive than that on the face and needs richer, less irritating creams.

Serums

These deliver concentrated bursts of hydrating or anti-ageing ingredients to the skin. Use two to three minutes before your normal moisturizer so they can be absorbed.

Pore strips

Help clear blackheads and reduce blocked and open pores.

Blackhead extractor

Only to be used after steaming or deep cleansing the skin.

Spot sticks

Usually containing antiseptic ingredients like witch hazel, salicylic acid or tea tree oil, these help fight minor blemishes.

This page: serum capsules; blackhead extractor. Main image, first row: heavy moisturizer; under-eye cream. Second row: night cream; light cream moisturizer; anti-ageing cream. Third row: light gel moisturizer; lip balm.

what it all means

Confused by the terms on your products? Here's how to break through the lingo.

ALPHA-HYDROXY ACIDS:
These slough off dead skin cells to reveal smoother, younger-looking skin underneath.

ANTIOXIDANTS:
Ingredients like vitamin C, A and E, green tea, copper, grapeseed and kinetin help skin by neutralizing molecules called free radicals that destroy skin cells.

AQUA:
Normally the number-one product on ingredient listings, it's plain water and it's vital for healthy skin.

BETA-HYDROXY ACIDS:
These work in the same way as alpha-hydroxy acids but are less irritating to the skin; the most common one used is salicylic acid, which also fights bacteria on the skin.

BOTANICALS:
Ingredients from a natural source (normally plants) believed to have healing or regenerating powers on the skin – common ones include aloe vera, gingko and ginseng.

COENZYME Q10:
A nutrient found in every cell of our body, this is also a good wrinkle-buster.

EMOLLIENTS:
Found in moisturizers, these help protect the skin by reinforcing the moisture barrier in the lower layer of the skin.

ESSENTIAL OILS *:
Most commonly used in aromatherapy, these are plant oils used to scent products but also as ingredients – lavender is commonly used in skin creams as it soothes irritation.

* If you are pregnant or epileptic, check with your doctor before using these.

HUMECTANTS:

Friend of the emollient, these attract moisture to the skin from the air.

HYPOALLERGENICS:

Ingredients shown to be least likely to cause allergic reactions.

LIPOSOMES:

These aren't ingredients but ways to deliver ingredients like vitamins deeper into the skin.

MATTIFYERS:

Ingredients like witch hazel or cornstarch that soak up oil on the skin.

NON-COMEDOGENICS:

Ingredients shown to be less likely to block pores.

RETINOLS:

Another word for products made from vitamin A, these are powerful antioxidants and some (the prescription-only Retin A and Retinova) have been shown to dramatically reduce skin damage from ultraviolet rays.

SUN PROTECTION FACTORS:

The most important ingredient in any skincare product, they screen out harmful and ageing ultraviolet rays.

what type of skin do you have?

To create perfect skin you have to treat each individual cell within it perfectly. You need to know if the cell needs more water, less oil – or just leaving alone to calm down and stop getting hot and bothered. The only way you're going to do this is to know your skin type. Now, you may think you know this already, but many of us are wrong. For starters, skin types change with age, so oily skin in your teens doesn't mean oily skin in your twenties, thirties or forties. Skin types can also change with the seasons, as temperatures affect the levels of oil and water in the skin; they can change with your diet, and even according to the time of the month. So to truly know your skin type, you have to reassess it regularly. Doing so is easy – just answer the following questions and see which letter you choose most often.

1 First thing in the morning, take a look at your face in bright light. What do you see?

a) It's shiny with noticeable blackheads

b) It looks flaky and feels taut

c) My forehead, chin and nose are shiny, the rest is tight and flaky

d) It's very pale, and there are occasional red or flaky patches

e) The surface is dull, I'm low on colour and there are noticeable lines and wrinkles

2 Wash your skin with some plain soap and water. Wait for about 20 minutes – now what do you notice?

a) It looks less shiny

b) It looks and feels tighter – plus it's gone a grey colour

c) It's less shiny on my nose and forehead but now my cheeks feel dreadful

d) It's itchy, red and flaky – thanks a lot

e) My lines and wrinkles are even more noticeable – but I've got some colour back into my skin tone

3 Do you get spots?

a) Yes, I'm prone to blackheads, whiteheads or big red ones that hurt

b) Not really – only around my period or if I use thick moisturizer

c) Only on my nose, forehead and chin

d) Yes, but they're red rather than whiteheads – or I get rashes

e) Very rarely

4 Look at your nose and the area around it – what do you notice most?

a) Blackheads, whiteheads and oil

b) Flaky patches and redness around my nostrils

c) That my nose and cheeks look like they're from two different faces – my nose is shiny, my cheeks are dull

d) There are lots of little red veins and high colour on my cheeks

e) I've lots of open pores

5 Take your index finger and lightly press your cheek upwards. What do you see?

a) Nothing really

b) I get loads of tiny lines like crepe paper that vanish when I stop

c) Some lines appear, but when I stop pressing they go away

d) The area goes white, then red or it feels hot

e) I get folds of skin forming and it takes a while to snap back to normal

6 Now get a magnifying mirror – or at least stand in some really bright natural light. Look at your pores – what are they like?

a) Big, black and shiny

b) Practically non-existent

c) Big on my nose, chin or forehead, but non-existent elsewhere

d) Practically non-existent

e) Large but clear – there's no oil there

7 Apply your make-up as normal in the morning, then at lunchtime take a long hard look in the mirror. What's happened?

a) What's left of it is shiny, but most of it has disappeared

b) It's gone blotchy and flaky

c) My cheeks aren't so bad, but my nose is shiny

d) My skin looks a bit red and irritated

e) It's settled on the lines of my face or looks dry

RESULTS

Mostly A's
You have oily skin – turn to page 37 to find out how to treat it

Mostly B's
You have dry skin – turn to page 41 to find out how to treat it

Mostly C's
You have combination skin – turn to page 47 to find out how to treat it

Mostly D's
You have sensitive skin – turn to page 51 to find out how to treat it

Mostly E's
You have maturing skin – turn to page 55 to find out how to treat it

oily skin

'Treating oily skin is a matter of trying to reduce oil production and keeping the pores clean to prevent stretching and oxidation'

What are the characteristics?

On average, the pores on the face of someone with oily skin produce around two grams of sebum a year. The thin layer of oil this creates on the skin leads to a shiny surface, open pores (which stretch as oil accumulates in them), blackheads (which occur when that oil is exposed to air and oxidizes) and whiteheads (which occur when dead skin cells stick in the oil and degrade). Sometimes the pores create acne too, but don't assume that if you have oily skin, acne follows — research seems to show that the oil in acne-prone skin is thicker and more likely to clog the pores than normal. There are various reasons for oily skin. It's often hormonal, which is why teens are prone or why skin can become oilier before your period; it can also be triggered by high humidity. Finally, oily skin can actually be caused by poor skincare. If you strip the top layers of the skin of too much moisture, the lower levels produce more oil to counteract this. On skin which produces higher oil levels anyway, this leads to serious shine.

How to care for oily skin

Treating oily skin is therefore a matter of trying to reduce oil production and keeping the pores clean to prevent stretching and oxidation. To many people with oily skin this means a routine of harsh cleansers and facial scrubs, but these just create that panic response. Instead, use light foaming cleansers, which have enough power to break through the oil and grime on the skin without irritation. The added bonus of these is that the action of rubbing them onto the skin (particularly if you remove them with a flannel or soft cloth) removes dead skin cells that can block pores and lead to whiteheads. People with acne-prone skin can try medicated washes or those based on salicylic acid (a plant-based ingredient which fights bacteria on the skin and helps prevent pore blockage).

You may think that you should follow up with a toner. The hype says toners close the pores and lower oil production, but it's not true. Most toners actually irritate the skin, making it swell, which makes the pores look smaller, but the oil production stays the same. In fact, the time to tackle oil production is when you moisturize. Many people with oily skin feel they don't need moisturizer, but that is also not true – you could still be lacking in water and by replenishing this you'll make the skin look plumper and healthier. This is particularly true of the neck, chest and around the eyes – all areas that dry out easily. Gel-based moisturizers (preferably those that are marked oil-free or non-comedogenic) will therefore help your skin look its best.

But I promised you oil control, didn't I? Well, many beauty companies are now adding ingredients such as witch hazel, salicylic acid and talcum to moisturizers for oily skin. These soak up sebum on the skin's surface and can keep you shine-free for up to eight hours. Look for products that claim to be 'mattifying' or 'shine controllers' and watch your skin thrive.

cleansing facial for oily skin

This is the perfect once-a-week treat for oily skin.

1 Cleanse. Apply a foaming (but soap-free) cleanser to your face, then, using a soft flannel, gently rub the whole face in circular motions. This will break down oil and grime on the skin's surface, while the movement will exfoliate any dead cells.

2 Steam your face. Boil some water and pour it into a large bowl. After the really hot steam has dispersed, lower your face over the bowl (keeping it at least 10 inches off the water). Put a towel over your head and stay put for up to 10 minutes.

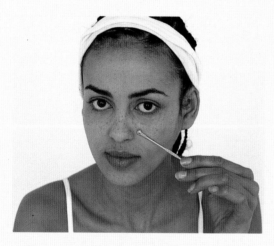

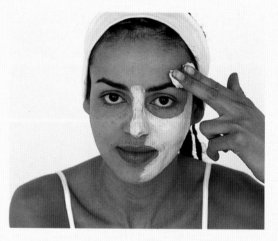

3 Use a blackhead extractor or wrap clean tissue around the tips of your fingers and gently apply pressure round the sides of the blackheads. Move the tissue regularly. When you've finished apply a little witch hazel or tea tree oil.

4 Apply a clay-based face mask. This will help draw out any more impurities and deep-cleanse the skin. If the mask makes your face sting then it's too harsh for your skin: try our strawberry-based mask (see page 39) instead. If you have any blemishes, apply a spot treatment based on salicylic acid or benzoyl peroxide, then apply your moisturizer as normal.

TOP 5 TIPS FOR OILY SKIN

• Only cleanse twice a day. More often will trigger that panic response.

• If shine still slips through, blotting paper is great for mopping up excess oil.

• Ensure all your products – even your make-up – are oil-free.

• Cut down on fast food. No, grease doesn't cause grease, but studies show that the iodine in fast food can contribute to spots on oily skin.

• If you get painful red spots, a little lavender oil dabbed on the skin will help reduce inflammation in minutes. In emergencies, whiteheads can be dried out with toothpaste.

YOUR 5 KEY PRODUCTS
Foaming cleanser
Oil-free moisturizer
Clay mask
Blotting papers
Spot stick

MAKE YOUR FACE MASK

Strawberries have great astringent properties and will help cleanse oily skin without irritation. For an easy face mask blend together the following ingredients:

½ tsp lemon juice
1 egg white
1 tsp honey
½ cup strawberries

Leave the mask on cleansed skin for 10 minutes and rinse off.

dry skin

'The moisturizer you use can be the product that makes the difference between dry skin and perfect skin'

What are the characteristics?

If you've got dry skin you probably never really feel comfortable in your face – it'll be tight and look dull and grey. It's often flaky too (particularly around the nose) and develops lots of tiny fine lines which can make you look older than you are. Dry skin occurs when the protective barrier of oil in the lower level of the skin starts to break down and water evaporates from the skin into the air. A number of things can destroy this barrier: it can be genetic; central heating and cold temperatures are common causes (which is why beauty companies sell more moisturizer in January than in any other month); or you can lose skin oils if you're on a diet too low in fat.

The problem with dry skin is that it will make you old before your time; not only is it prone to natural wrinkling but UV rays penetrate deeper into dehydrated skin, increasing sun damage. Getting those moisture levels back up to scratch is therefore vital for your looks.

How to care for dry skin

To care effectively for dry skin means ensuring the products that you use contain no drying ingredients like alcohol or soap. Instead, they should contain ingredients that put something back into your skin. Choose creamy or milky cleansers that will add moisture and leave a fine film that boosts skin protection. If you must use soap, choose glycerine-based ones that also coat the skin.

You also need to exfoliate. One of the reasons why dry skin tends to look dull is that its cell renewal process has been slowed and dead skin cells stick to the surface of the skin. Using a cleanser with alpha-hydroxy acids can help beat this. Apply them every day for a week, then rest for one or two weeks – using them too often can be harsh. In between, use a gentle facial scrub to remove dead skin cells and boost skin tone.

The moisturizer you use can make the difference between dry and perfect skin.

Moisturizers use two types of ingredient to hydrate the skin – humectants that attract moisture to the skin and emollients that help reinforce that protective barrier. Choose products that include both. Look for ingredients such as hyaluronic acid, glycerine or sorbitol (which are humectants) and lactic acid, collagen, petrolatum and lanolin (which are emollients). Choosing moisturizers that are high in water will also help the skin look and feel hydrated. Apply the moisturizer at least twice daily – more if your skin still feels dry and taut.

Finally, as most cases of dry skin are caused by environmental factors, try to minimize the chances of dehydration in your daily life. Invest in a humidifier to keep water levels in the air high and cut the amount the atmosphere sucks from your skin. In winter months, try to keep your skin covered, and apply moisturizer, lip balm and hand cream before you go out. The more water you manage to keep in, the less you have to try and put back.

hydrating facial for dry skin

Dry skin needs a lot more care than most other skin types, so do this facial once or twice a week until moisture levels are boosted.

1 Exfoliate. Using your gentle facial scrub, rub the skin in a circular motion. Concentrate on areas like the nose and forehead. Some scrubs can dry the skin out, so rinse well.

2 Cleanse the skin with a milky cleanser. Doing this after the exfoliation will help remove any deep-down grime rather than just polishing the dead skin cells on the surface. Wipe it away with cotton wool: it's less absorbent than tissues and so will leave more protection on the skin.

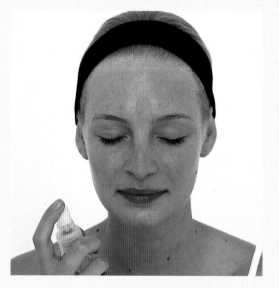

3 Spritz or splash your skin. Toners are a no-no on dry skin as they will dehydrate it. Instead, freshen up your face with a spritz of facial mist or a splash of cool water. Absorb any excess afterwards but don't completely dry the skin.

4 Now apply a hydrating mask. Look for emollient or humectant ingredients in these – or try our recipe on page 45 which is packed with natural moisture givers. Leave this for 10 to 15 minutes, then rinse off. Again, leave the face damp.

5 Apply your moisturizer. The best way to do this is by patting the skin with your fingers – this helps bring blood to the skin's surface which will help hydrate it from within.

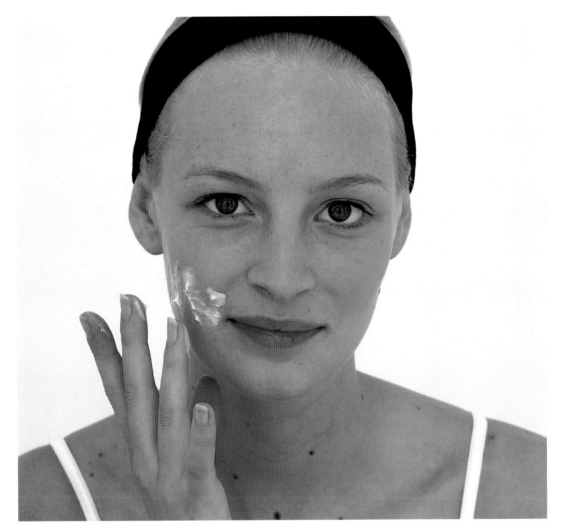

TOP 5 TIPS FOR DRY SKIN

• Only cleanse your skin once at the end of the day. This will remove dirt and grime but will prevent further drying. In the morning, a splash of water and some moisturizer are all you need.

• Exfoliation is essential for dry skin. When choosing your facial scrub, avoid any made from seeds or salt – these can have sharp edges which may tear dry skin, increasing moisture loss.

• Never expose your skin to really hot water. It dries out parched skin.

• Never dry your skin completely. One of the best ways to hydrate dry skin is just to pat it with the towel after washing, then apply moisturizer to seal in that extra moisture.

• Increase your intake of oily fish or take a supplement of essential fatty acids. One of the main tell-tale signs of deficiency of these essential nutrients is dry, flaking skin.

YOUR 5 KEY PRODUCTS

Creamy cleanser
Exfoliating scrub
Rich moisturizer
Facial mist
Moisturizing mask

MAKE YOUR FACE MASK

Honey and avocados are particularly rich in moisturizing properties. For the perfect skin food mash together the following ingredients:

½ avocado
¼ cup honey

Apply to your face and leave for five minutes before removing with a flannel and some tepid water.

combination skin

'For the ultimate blackhead-buster turn to the pore strip – little sticky pads which you place over blocked pores and then pull off, gunk and all'

What are the characteristics?

Combination skin is normally a mix of oily skin in the centre of the face (an area commonly called the T-zone) plus dry or normal skin on the cheeks. Exactly which areas are affected often changes with age – teens find their forehead and nose are big problems and this tends to be caused by the hormones flying around in puberty; older women find chins sometimes break out, too, and this is often linked to increased stress levels.

Outside the oily zone the state of the skin tends to depend a lot on your skincare. Using products to tackle the grease dramatically dries out the cheeks, chest and eyes. Tackling combination skin is therefore a matter of balance.

How to care for combination skin

Your aim should be to treat the problem on one area of the face without harming the skin of the other areas. Your first step is cleansing. It's best to avoid harsh cleansers that are formulated for oily skin or milky cleansers formulated for dry skin and instead use a moisturizing cleansing bar or facial wash. The foaming action of these will help strip through the oil on the greasier parts of your skin but won't dehydrate the cheeks at the same time. After cleansing, use a gentle exfoliator. Many women with combination skin find they tend to get spots around their nose as the dry flakes of skin from their cheeks stick to the oily areas and so cause blockages. Gentle exfoliation will go a long way to help reduce this.

Exfoliation will loosen blackheads, but for the ultimate blackhead-buster turn to the pore strip – little sticky pads which you place over blocked pores and then pull off. These are perfect for combination skins as they allow you to focus your treatment on the affected area. For best results use the strips every day for three days, then reduce it to just once a week.

The final step in your skincare programme is your moisturizer, and here you do need to pander a little to your different skin types. During the day, when beating the shine is what counts, you should use mattifying products to soak up the sebum produced in your T-zone without drying out your cheeks.

Many companies now sell mattifying products using ingredients like witch hazel, talcum or cornstarch to soak up oil without irritation. At night, choose oil-free creams or light moisture lotions which will supply your cheeks with extra hydration without over-stimulating the oil in your T-zone.

balancing facial for combination skin

This once-a-week treat intensively tackles both the dry and oily areas of your skin.

1 Cleanse your face using a moisturizing facial bar or a foaming cleanser. This will effectively target the oil on the greasy skin of the T-zone, without removing any of the moisture from the dry skin on your cheeks.

2 Exfoliate to avoid flakes of dry skin clogging pores. Using a gentle facial scrub or a flannel, rub the cheeks lightly. Go more intensely when tackling the greasy areas of the face to help loosen blackheads.

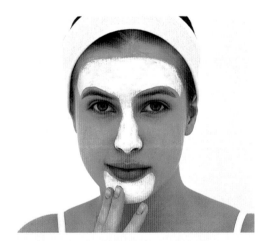

3 Boil a kettle of water and pour some into a large bowl. Add four drops of rosewater to the bowl – this hydrates the skin and will prevent the steam drying out the cheeks while it tackles the nose. After the hot steam has dispersed, lower your face over the bowl, keeping it 10 inches off the water. Put a towel over your head and stay put for up to 10 minutes.

4 On big pamper sessions like this one, go for the double mask. Shop around for a hydrating moisture mask you apply to your cheeks and throat and a clay-based mask for the oily areas. Leave the masks on for 10 minutes and rinse with tepid water before applying your normal light moisturizer. Alternatively, try our mask on page 49.

TOP 5 TIPS FOR COMBINATION SKIN

• Don't scrub oily areas – this irritates the skin and increases oil production.

• Don't treat your whole face the same. Your T-zone will require cleansing twice a day, while the cheeks only need doing once. It's vice versa with moisturizing.

• After using pore strips, apply tea tree oil to your nose. It will reduce redness and cut bacteria levels in the pores.

• Avoid leave-in hair conditioners. Ingredients in these block the forehead's pores, making already greasy skin worse.

• Don't forget eye creams: you may need to avoid rich moisturizers on your cheeks, but you shouldn't skip them on the delicate skin around your eyes.

YOUR 5 KEY PRODUCTS
Cleansing bars
Pore strips
Exfoliating scrub
Oil-free moisturizer
Eye cream

MAKE YOUR FACE MASK

A rose-based mask is an excellent balancing treatment for combination skin. Use the following ingredients:

1 rose
1 tbsp rosewater
1 tbsp natural yoghurt
1 tbsp honey

Wash the rose petals in water. Soak for a few minutes and then crush them in a bowl. Add the rosewater, yoghurt and honey. Mix well and apply to the skin for five minutes. Rinse off with tepid water.

sensitive skin

'Natural products may suit you as they often contain calming ingredients like camomile, cornflower, milk and liquorice'

What are the characteristics?

If you have sensitive skin you will find that skincare or make-up products are very hard to use, creating itching, flaking, reddening or flushing. Eighty per cent of women think they have sensitive skin, though in reality only 10 to 20 per cent show the true characteristics. If you're one of them, you're likely to have fair skin or red hair, be prone to flushing easily (red veins and high colour are signs of potential sensitivity) or suffer other types of allergy like hay fever or asthma, as these cause the release of histamines which make your skin more reactive. Stabilizing the skin and treating it with products that won't cause these reactions are the way to get it looking good.

How to care for sensitive skin

First, eliminate any unnecessary products from your skincare regime. The average woman uses five or six skincare products, so exposing her skin to more than 100 chemicals a day – and you could be sensitive to any one of these. All you really need for good skin is a cleanser, a moisturizer with a sunscreen and, depending on your age, an eye cream. Everything else is superfluous – and, in the case of harsh products like alcohol-based cleansers and toners, retinols and alpha-hydroxy acids, may cause more problems than they solve.

Second, make sure you avoid products containing ingredients most likely to cause sensitivity. These are usually fragrances, colours and preservatives (particularly formaldehyde), though technically you could be sensitive to anything. One relatively painless way of reducing the risk is to use only those products from ranges that say they are hypoallergenic. Natural products may suit you, as they often contain calming ingredients like camomile, cornflower, milk and liquorice.

Third, treat your skin with care. Make sure you cleanse gently to remove make-up at the end of the day as reactions tend to occur when you overexpose your skin to any product. Use very light, creamy cleansers or, preferably, facial wipes, which minimize your contact with product ingredients. Restrict cleansing to once a day to help maintain the skin's own protection. Use a specialist eye make-up remover, as facial cleansers may include ingredients that will irritate your eyes.

Moisturizing is important: the drier the skin, the more prone it is to sensitivity. Apply a light moisturizer twice daily. To treat other problems like ageing or spots, do it just once a week and stick to one product. If your skin reacts, water down the dose by mixing it with a moisturizer or an over-the-counter hydrocortisone cream. If you still get a reaction, stop.

calming facial for sensitive skin

Once a month, treat your skin to a facial designed to calm and stabilize. There aren't many steps here as the aim is to reduce your exposure to too many ingredients.

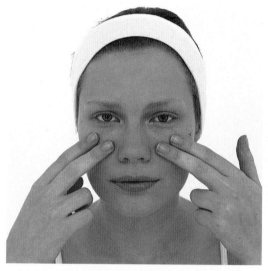

1 Camomile is incredibly calming, so for this session we're going to skip your cleanser and opt for a soothing camomile wash instead. Soak four camomile teabags in hot water. Once the water has cooled to warm, splash your face with this 20 to 30 times.

2 While your skin is still damp, stroke or tap the skin rapidly in downward motions. This helps drain away fluids and toxins under the skin's surface – and the fewer toxins there are in your system, the less chance there is of allergic reactions occurring.

3 Apply a hydrating face mask from a hypoallergenic range, or try our soothing moisturizing mask on page 53. As sensitive eyes can often feel red and itchy, give them a treat by applying some cotton-wool pads soaked in the camomile mixture of Step 1. Relax for five to ten minutes, then wash off the mask with tepid water. Stroke a soft cloth gently across the face to remove any excess. Don't rub the skin – it will only make it redder. Finish off with a cooling gel moisturizer. For ultimate soothing power, pop the gel in the fridge before you apply it.

TOP 5 TIPS FOR SENSITIVE SKIN

• Use products with fewer than 10 ingredients to reduce the risk of coming across something you're allergic to. Research has shown that applying too many ingredients to the skin can send the skin's immune system into overdrive.

• Wear sunscreen. Choose one that contains physical rather than chemical blocks like titanium dioxide and is less likely to cause an allergic reaction.

• Alternate products. The skin tends to become sensitized to things it encounters often. Find two different products and alternate every few weeks.

• Read labels. If you know you're allergic to a particular ingredient, avoid it. Bubble baths can contain chemical sunscreens to prevent them fading; nail varnish contains formaldehyde, which is a common cause of itchy eyes.

• If you're really allergic, use only water and hydrocortisone cream for six months. Introduce gentle products one at a time.

YOUR 5 KEY PRODUCTS
Facial wipes
Eye make-up remover
Light moisturizer
Chemical-free sunscreen
Hydrocortisone cream

MAKE YOUR FACE MASK

This soothing mask helps reduce irritation. It's also great on sun-damaged skin. Use the following ingredients:

1 cup natural yoghurt
½ cup oatmeal

Blend the yoghurt and oatmeal together. Mix well and apply to the skin for 10 minutes. Rinse off with warm water.

maturing skin

'The neck and chest are some of the first areas to show ageing, yet most of us ignore them'

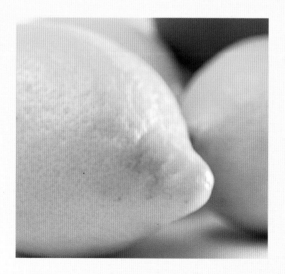

What are the characteristics?

If you're in your twenties or thirties you may be surprised to find yourself in this category – surely maturing means you're in your forties? Well, not necessarily. What maturing skin means is that for some reason (be it sun damage, smoking, or high levels of stress) your skin is starting to 'act old' – and this may have nothing to do with what it says on your birth certificate. By 'acting old', we mean that your skin may be starting to lose its natural glow or its elasticity. It's likely to be developing more lines than you would like or becoming a slave to open pores. These things can begin as early as your mid-twenties or thirties (probably due to those trips to Spain as a child). However, you can slow them down.

How to care for maturing skin

If you do have maturing skin you probably think cleansing is the least of your worries – after all, you're past the greasy, spotty stage. However, cleansing the skin with the right products can actually help reduce some of the signs of ageing. Choose a cleanser that contains alpha- or beta-hydroxy acids, as these help increase cell replacement which slows on maturing skin, reducing its radiance; they also help clean and shrink open pores that become more noticeable as we age. The use of AHA/BHA cleansers also removes the need for a toner, which can dry maturing skin further. Once a week, use a gentle exfoliating scrub (or a peel-off face mask). This will remove dead cells and keep the skin glowing.

In terms of moisturizing, you should be aiming to replace oils and water (the more hydrated the skin is, the less noticeable lines and wrinkles are), so choose rich creams that provide oil and attract moisture to the skin (see the section on dry skin for more advice on this). When applying moisturizer, don't make the mistake of stopping when you get to your chin – the neck and chest are some of the first areas to show ageing, yet most of us ignore them. It will also help to choose products that incorporate age-fighting ingredients – like vitamin A (also referred to as retinols), vitamin C, coenzyme Q10, kinetin and copper. Which you choose is up to you, as they all do the same thing – fight molecules called free radicals that destroy healthy skin cells, collagen and elastin. Use these in your moisturizer or try serums which deliver intensive bursts of nutrients to the skin.

And, finally, always wear sunscreen. None of the rest is worth doing if you don't – even in winter it can take just 20 minutes of unprotected exposure to damage the skin. We'll talk more about sunscreen later, but for now suffice it to say that if you want to help ageing skin, your moisturizer must contain sunscreen of at least SPF15.

firming facial for maturing skin

This once-a-week facial hydrates intensely, but also uses massage techniques to boost circulation and tighten and firm the skin.

1 Cleanse the skin using a milky cleanser, applying it directly onto your face with your fingers. Leave it to sink in for a few seconds, then, using circular movements (always moving up the face), massage it in. Remove with cotton wool in the same fashion. This will increase circulation to the skin.

2 Starting at your chin, move around the edge of the jaw and face, lightly tapping the skin 10 to 20 times at points an inch apart. Do the same around the eyes. This will help boost circulation and reduce puffiness, creating a firmer look.

3 Apply an exfoliating mask. This will get rid of dead skin cells but is more hydrating than a facial scrub alone (try a peel-off cucumber mask or our sugar recipe on page 59). Apply tightening cucumber pads (or slices of the real thing) to your eyes and relax. Rinse off, finishing by splashing the face 10 to 20 times with cold water. This boosts circulation, ready for the treatments to come.

4 Apply a vitamin serum, again using upward stroking movements but this time from the neck. Slap the underside of your chin 20 times.

5 Finish with a thick coat of rich moisturizer. Leave this to soak in for five minutes, then remove any excess with cotton wool.

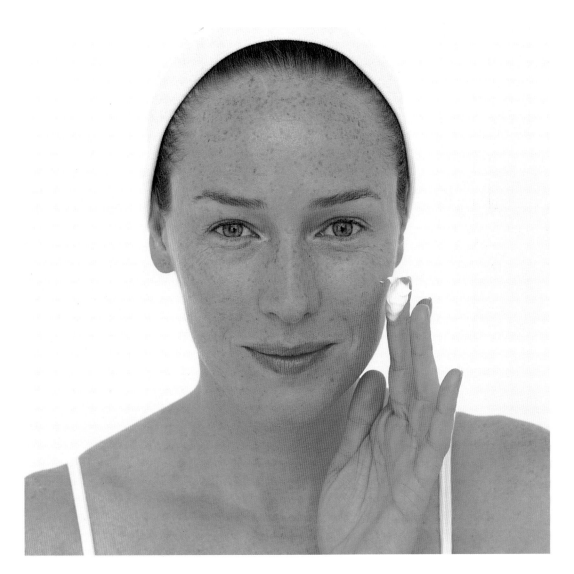

TOP 5 TIPS FOR MATURING SKIN

• Rich moisturizers are great for maturing skin, but if you start to break out in spots, your moisturizer is too rich. Alternate with a lighter brand.

• Don't stop skincare at your chin – your neck gives away your age faster than your face ever can. Ditto your hands – always rub a little of whatever you're using on your face on those too.

• Use a special eye cream daily: eyes are the first place to show ageing and need specialist treatment.

• Never drag the skin while removing make-up or putting on moisturizer When the skin is already under threat from ageing, pulling or folding the skin adds to the pressure. Do everything lightly.

• Boost your intake of antioxidant vitamins by aiming for seven portions of fruit and vegetables a day. These not only help fight ageing, but also help your skin to create its own sun protection, which will fight any UV rays that get through your sunscreen.

YOUR 5 KEY PRODUCTS
Alpha-hydroxy acid cleanser
Rich moisturizer
Vitamin serum
Eye cream
SPF30+ sunscreen

MAKE YOUR FACE MASK
Sugar is a great skin exfoliant as it removes dead skin cells without drying the skin. Mix the following ingredients together to brighten older skin:

2 tbsp sugar
3 tbsp warm water

Melt the sugar in some warm water (in neat form sugar granules can cause tiny tears in the skin, which allow moisture to leak out). Apply to the face, leave for five minutes, then very gently massage around the skin. Rinse well.

seven deadly skin sins

All the skincare in the world won't help if you don't tackle the factors that destroy your skin. Here are the seven deadly skin sins and solutions to help you beat them.

Sun

Did you know that if you protected your skin from the sun you wouldn't get a wrinkle on your face until you were 60? Exposing your face to sunlight is the fastest way to age your skin. When ultraviolet light hits the skin's surface it produces molecules called free radicals which destroy healthy cells. They're particularly fond of collagen and elastin – the two ingredients that help keep skin firm and elastic. The further the collagen and elastin degrade, the faster wrinkles appear on your skin. In peak sunlight, collagen and elastin damage can occur in as little as three minutes.

The good news is that you can prevent sun damage quite simply – by wearing sunscreen whenever you leave the house. For day-to-day wear SPF15 is enough, but if you're on the beach or sightseeing on holiday, wear SPF30 or above. Australian research has shown that this does more than just protect against further damage. Wearing high-factor (SPF30+) sunscreen every day also helps reverse past damage, as the skin gets the chance to repair itself.

To really protect your skin, you need to use enough to fill a shot glass to cover your body and about a teaspoonful on your face. Apply this at least half an hour before you go into the sun, as it takes this long for the ingredients to be absorbed, and then reapply every 90 minutes.

Finally, stay out of the sun – or at least stay covered up between the peak hours of 11 to 3 o'clock; even the strongest sunscreen only filters out 99 per cent of rays and sunbathing in these hours can still cause damage to your skin.

Smoking

After exposure to sunlight, smoking is the next most damaging thing you can do to your skin. First, the nicotine in cigarettes constricts the blood vessels of the face, making your skin look grey or sallow. Next, an ingredient called acetaldehyde goes to work, attacking the fibres in your skin that hold it together. Finally, a chemical reaction occurs which creates a protein that causes the destruction of collagen and elastin. Add to this the constant creasing and wrinkling of the eyes due to smoke irritation (you might not even realize you do it, but you do) and the pursing of the lips as you inhale and it's easy to see why the average smoker looks around 10 years older than a non-smoker of the same age.

The solution is simple – quit. Studies show that quitting before you are 30 returns your body to the level of a non-smoker within 10 years, and this goes for your skin as well as your lungs. Now, we know that quitting smoking isn't as easy as one, two, three, but it is possible with dedication, perseverance and a methodical approach. Our top tips should help you crack it:

- **Choose a day:** The day before, throw away anything that reminds you of smoking: cigarettes, matches, ashtrays. It will also help to wash curtains and hoover carpets and furniture to get the smell from your house.
- **Change your routine:** Avoid activities you associate with smoking, or do them differently. If you always light up with a glass of wine, for example, drink lager or diet cola instead. If you smoke in front of your favourite soap, record the episodes for a couple of weeks to stop your need to habit-puff.
- **Eat lots of fruit and vegetables:** This helps neutralize the nicotine in your system faster and reduces withdrawal cravings. If cravings do strike, sniff black pepper oil. Studies have shown that it stops them in their tracks.

Alcohol

While nicotine constricts blood vessels, alcohol dilates them and in sensitive skins this can lead to broken veins and high colour. Alcohol also contains acetaldehyde which attacks skin fibres, reducing firmness and elasticity. It dehydrates the skin – as little as two drinks a day have been shown to dry the skin enough to make wrinkles more prominent. Finally, alcohol destroys vitamin C, one of the most important nutrients for healthy skin functioning. Alcohol-related problems can occur after two drinks, so try not to drink more than this a day. Aim for three alcohol-free days a week and try to drink at least two glasses of water for every glass of alcohol.

Stress

Stress affects the skin in a number of ways. First, it increases levels of adrenal hormones like testosterone, which have been linked to the triggering of acne. In fact, stress is being blamed for the increase in so-called adult acne in career women. The stress hormones also cause blood flow to be directed away from the surface of the skin to your limbs and major organs (in case you need to run away). This means that your skin doesn't get all the nutrients it needs and takes on a grey pallor. To add insult to injury, you can't repair these problems with skincare as effectively when you're stressed; studies show that stressed skin doesn't absorb products as well as relaxed skin. If stress does hit, knowing how to keep calm will help your skin survive. Try sniffing lavender or adding a few drops to your bathwater (it has been shown to increase relaxation levels in the brain); exercising, which releases calming chemicals into the body; or deep breathing, which slows the heart rate and triggers the production of more calming chemicals.

Lack of sleep

Not getting the right amount of sleep is a disaster for your skin. Night-time is when the skin repairs itself – you build new cells and replace collagen and elastin damaged by the day's exposure to sun and pollution. The skin is also more absorbent at night, which means it takes in treatments more effectively – in fact, research shows that up to 25 per cent more of some vitamin treatments enter the skin at night compared to during the day. Lack of sleep cuts these benefits and causes side effects of its own, such as dark circles, sallowness and puffiness under the eyes, as the skin diverts blood to fuel the tired brain and other organs. It can even cause spots, as studies show that people pick at their skin more when they're tired and this can introduce bacteria.

In an ideal world we'd all get the ideal amount of sleep for our bodies every night, though this doesn't necessarily mean eight hours. Sleep experts admit that some of us do thrive on four hours a night, while others needs at least 10 to feel their best. To find out how much is right for you, go to bed when you're tired and get up when you wake up for a week, and calculate how long you spent in bed. Divide the week's total by seven – that's your optimum sleepload. If you find it hard to get to sleep, there are things that can help. Researchers have found that taking a bath with the water at a temperature of 38 to 41 degrees Centigrade promotes the production of sleep hormones; add some lavender or melissa oils to the water and you'll compound these benefits. Milky drinks can also induce sleepiness, and if all else fails, try some herbal help with supplements of valerian or passionflower, which have been shown to assist people to fall asleep faster and stay asleep longer.

Pollution

Pollution and harmful chemicals are another cause of free radicals in the skin and can contribute to ageing. On average we breathe in two grams of pollution and eat five kilograms each of food additives and pesticides every year. Avoiding pollution is tricky. However, you can help fight internal damage by increasing your intake of fresh fruit and vegetables, which contain antioxidants to fight the damage, and also by choosing organic produce where possible.

Lack of exercise

Physical activity helps boost skin tone by increasing the amount of oxygen in your blood and reducing the amount of toxins that build up under your skin. It also boosts skin health by increasing your tolerance to stress and helping you sleep – studies show that people who work out fall asleep faster and stay asleep longer than those who don't. For optimum skin health, do three sets of 20 minutes' exercise a week. This should be anything that makes you out of breath and starts your heart pumping faster – try running, swimming, cycling, even dancing, just so long as it gets you moving.

eat your way to better skin

So far we've mainly discussed things to put on the outside to make you look better. But what you put inside your body is as important when it comes to creating perfect skin. Here's what you need.

Vitamin A

Not only is it a powerful antioxidant, but vitamin A also helps your skin produce keratin (a substance that strengthens skin cells, maximizing their protective role) and proteins that help with cell regeneration. If you're lacking in it, your skin may be drier and flakier than normal. You can get your daily dose from fruits and vegetables that are high in an ingredient called beta-carotene, which your body turns into vitamin A. Beta-carotene is found in the highest quantities in orange fruits and vegetables like carrots, peaches, pumpkin and sweet potatoes.

Vitamin C

Collagen is one of the most important substances in the structure of the skin – it is what keeps it firm and well toned. To feed collagen you need vitamin C. There are two reasons for this: first, the antioxidant action of vitamin C helps fight the free radicals that destroy collagen; and second, vitamin C also contains substances called flavonoids that are essential for replenishing collagen. Vitamin C can be found in many fruits and vegetables – one of the richest sources is kiwi fruit. One kiwi contains the minimum recommended daily amount of vitamin C – pop four or five down in a day and you'll be dramatically boosting your skin health. Other great sources are oranges, red peppers, blueberries and melon.

Iron

Low iron levels in the body lead to reduced oxygen in the blood and this can be the cause of pale skin and pronounced dark circles under the eyes. In order to boost your iron levels you should include more lean red meat and plenty of dark green leafy vegetables in your diet.

Zinc

Zinc is a mineral that is vital for healing the skin and it's also been shown to reduce acne. You'll find high levels of zinc in foods such as shellfish, hard crumbly cheeses, nuts and seeds.

Essential fatty acids

Dry skin often occurs when women start on low-fat diets and the lack of essential fatty acids is the reason. One of the most frequent symptoms of a deficiency of fatty acids is dry, scaly skin. EFAs are commonly found in oily fish, nuts and seeds (which also contain high levels of another important skin nutrient, vitamin E).

Water

Water not only keeps skin cells plump, but every rejuvenating process in the skin needs water to fuel it. Without enough water in your skin you'll never recapture that healthy glow. Aim for at least eight glasses of water a day – but don't guzzle them all at once. Your body can only hold

so much water in one go – exceed that level and it will be flushed straight through your system. Aim for one glass an hour.

What you don't need

- **Salty foods:** These dehydrate the skin and are high in iodine. Dermatologists believe that this can trigger acne.
- **Caffeine:** Every cup of coffee needs three cups of water to process it through the system – this is often drawn from the skin. Caffeine increases the level of stress hormones, which can lead to poor skin health.
- **Hydrogenated fats:** Found in nearly all processed foods and margarines, these are believed to generate free radicals in the skin.

SKIN Q & A

Let us help you with your most common skincare questions.

Q: Do I have to use skincare products all from the same range?
A: You don't have to but it can improve your skin. Many ranges are designed to work together, with ingredients adjusted accordingly. This ensures that you get enough good ingredients like moisturizers and vitamins and reduces the risk of doubling up on potentially irritating ones like alpha-hydroxy acids or retinols. But if your skin feels fine when you mix and match, stick with it.

Q: What's the difference between day and night creams – and do I need both?
A: Generally, day creams are lighter, so more suitable for use under make-up, and nowadays normally include a sunscreen (which of course you don't need in a night cream). Whether you need both depends on your skin type. Dry or maturing skin may benefit from an intensive moisturizer at night.

Q: My spots aren't cleared up by cleansing or over-the-counter treatments. What now?
A: If an over-the-counter spot treatment doesn't work within six weeks, it's not going to. The thing with these treatments is that, while they are great at fighting superficial blemishes, they don't kill enough of the acne-causing bacteria to tackle more severe cases. But this doesn't mean you have to suffer. Doctors and dermatologists offer many other solutions to acne, starting with topical antibiotics which are applied to the skin to reduce bacteria levels. If your spots won't clear up, ask your doctor for help.

Q: I have great skin in summer, but come winter it gets uncomfortable, grey and flaky. What am I doing wrong?
A: Like your wardrobe, skincare is seasonal. Cold weather destroys the lipid layer that stops the skin drying out, while hot days create a build-up of oil and sunscreen that can lead to breakouts. As a general rule you should reassess your

skincare programme with the seasons. Follow the rules for your skin type, but bear in mind that you may need to cleanse more thoroughly in summer (and use lighter moisturizers), while in winter you might reduce cleansing on drier areas of the face and use thicker moisturizers or apply them more often.

Q: I always apply sunscreen – and I still burn. What am I doing wrong?

A: You're either not applying enough (see the skin sins section for more advice on this) or you're not using a sun protection factor high enough for your skin. Experts now say SPF15 (which allows you to stay out for 15 times longer than you could without cream without burning) is the minimum we should use, but for someone with fair skin who burns in minutes, this could still allow them only about an hour's safe exposure. The paler your skin, the higher you should go. Try switching to factor 30+.

Q: You've recommended alpha-hydroxy acid creams for my skin type, but I've heard they're bad for my skin.

A: When alpha-hydroxy acids came out they revolutionized beauty – the first over-the-counter treatment that actually seemed to make a difference to sun-damaged skin. So beauty companies put them in everything from moisturizers to lipstick – and we, as consumers, decided if a little was good, loads must be fantastic. But alpha-hydroxy acids aren't designed for overkill – they speed up cell renewal, but in doing so thin the skin. Research has shown that overuse of AHAs can thin the skin enough to make it prone to sun damage. This doesn't mean you should never use them, just that you should use them as intended – in just one product and ideally only for a week or two at a time, giving your skin time to repair in between. And you should always wear a sunscreen when you use them – but then, you should be wearing one anyway…

your hair

Understanding hair structure will help you get the best out of your hair. On average we each have 120,000 hairs on our head and to look good they all need to be in good condition – or at least disguised that way. The outside of the hair is called the cuticle. In strong, shiny hair this lies flat, allowing light to reflect from it (creating shine) and preventing moisture entering the hair (which causes frizzing) or leaving the internal hair shaft (which causes dryness). Many things can interfere with this cuticle, from harsh brushing to chemical processing, and these thin and weaken the hair shaft, so leading to brittleness. Your day-to-day haircare should therefore aim to smooth the cuticle and thicken or strengthen the hair shaft. How you do this depends on what type of hair you have (more on this later), and tailoring products to your type is as important for hair as it is for skin. But while beautiful hair may start with how you treat it day to day, it needn't end there. Colour and styling can enhance your looks – but, to ensure both do more good than harm, you need to know how to make them work for you.

the haircare equipment kit

Looking after your hair properly takes the right products – here's what you'll need.

Liquid shampoo

Cleans hair by lifting dirt and oil. It may surprise you how little you need for this – a blob the size of a 10p piece is enough for mid-length hair. Use less for short styles, more for long.

Dry shampoo

Great for absorbing oil between washes – a must for anyone with processed hair where roots need cleansing more often than ends. Apply, wait a few minutes, then brush well.

Rich conditioner

Best for day-to-day use, this should be applied for one to three minutes, then rinsed out well. Where you apply it and any magic ingredients you require depend on your hair type.

Leave-in conditioner

Used for fast fixes, these are normally lightweight and may offer UV protection – a good idea for coloured or curly hair.

Hot oil treatments

Oil moisturizes dry hair dramatically and in combination with heat is the best intensive treatment for hair.

Two-in-one shampoos

These combine shampoo and conditioner but they should be used only for short periods – they are not specialized enough for all-day, every-day haircare.

Wide-toothed comb

This is the only thing your hair should be touched with when it's wet.

Paddle brush

The best way to brush hair day to day. Nylon bristles suit every hair type except curly. For curly hair choose boar's-head bristles to prevent tangling.

Shine serum

Every hair type benefits from shine serum to help smooth the hair and give it an added gleam.

From left: 2-in-1 shampoo; conditioner; shampoo.

what it all means

Confused by the terms on your products? Here's how to break through the lingo.

CLARIFYING:
Uses ingredients specifically designed to strip through the hairstyling products' build-up on the hair. Good if you like using sprays, gels or waxes.

COLOUR ENHANCING:
Contains low levels of natural or chemical colorants to lift hair colour.

COLOUR PROTECTIVE:
Uses less aggressive detergents to prevent drying or colour stripping.

EXPRESS OR FAST-DRYING:
Limits the amount of moisture the hair absorbs, so making drying and styling time faster.

MOISTURIZING:
Uses less harsh detergent than traditional shampoo.

PH-BALANCED:
Stops the scalp from becoming too acidic or alkaline, in which conditions bacteria can thrive, causing irritation.

THICKENING SHAMPOOS:
Often use panthenol to thicken the hair shaft. Many also create an electrical charge within the hair to prevent strands sticking together, making hair look fuller.

VOLUMIZING SHAMPOOS:
Use thickening and firming agents to create lift in the hair.

what's in my product?

In days gone by haircare ingredients simply determined how a particular product smelt; now they can do everything from thicken to colour the hair. Here are some of the most common ingredients.

BEER:
This sticks to the hair's surface, thereby creating shine.

BOTANICALS:
Plant-based ingredients that act on the hair – for example, rosemary is said to help greasy scalps.

CAMOMILE:
A flower used in shampoos for blondes, it can lighten hair.

CLAY:
This deeply cleanses the hair and scalp. It's used in shampoo instead of potentially irritating detergents.

FRUIT ACIDS:
These boost shine and condition by changing the hair's pH balance.

FRUIT SUGARS:
These hydrate the hair by drawing water from the air.

PANTHENOL (B5):
This penetrates the hair shaft, causing it to swell and thicken.

PROTEIN:
Hair is made from a protein called keratin, but external proteins don't enhance this. Instead, they coat the hair, strengthening it and creating thickness.

VITAMINS:
Other than B5, these don't penetrate the hair; instead, like proteins, they coat it, making it look thicker.

ZINC PYRITHIONE:
The most common treatment for dandruff, it slows cell regeneration on the scalp.

what type of hair do you have?

As we've already explained, just like your skin, your hair has a type – and if you want it to look its best you need to treat it with products and techniques that suit its type. At one time, type simply meant either oily or dry, and shampoo dealt with these two things by either moisturizing dry hair or stripping the oil out of greasy hair. However, not all dry hair needed the same amount of moisturization and not all oily hair responded well to having that oil removed. What do we mean? Say you are a woman with curly hair (which is often dry), you're going to need a lot more moisture on your hair than a woman with chemically treated hair (which is dry at the ends but often greasier at the roots). Put intensive moisture on that hair and you'll just end up with limp, oily locks. As a result, the newest way to determine your hair type is not by deciding whether it's oily or dry but by analyzing its fundamental structure, which then tells you how to make the most of your tresses. So which type are you? To find out, answer the following questions until you get directed to your hair type.

Processed hair

Is your hair currently bleached, permed or more than 70 per cent highlights? If yes, you've got 'processed' hair and need to turn to the advice on page 79.

Curly hair

Is your hair naturally curly? If yes, then – surprise, surprise – you've got curly hair, and need to head to page 83 now.

Wavy hair

Is your hair wavy but not curly – that is, if you leave it to dry naturally, will it curl or wave either throughout or at the ends and have fullness but not definite curls? If so, head to the section on wavy hair, which you'll find on page 87.

Straight hair

Everyone who has got this far should have straight hair. This means when it's long it hangs flat, or if it's short it will hug your head and not bounce at the crown or curl at the nape of the neck. If you've got straight hair, you can solve your problems on page 91.

processed hair

What are the characteristics?

Colouring, perming and relaxing do enhance the look of hair, creating shade and depth – and also thickening the hair when they are applied. But they come at a cost. The chemicals used in these processes permanently alter the interior of the hair shaft and this can weaken the hair, making it prone to breaking, splitting or frizzing. Also, the disruption of the cuticle prevents light reflecting from the hair surface, making processed hair far less likely to shine than natural hair.

To check how damaged your hair is, take five or six strands and drop them in a glass of water, then tap them with your finger. If they sink, they're absorbing water – and this is a sign of damage. If they float then your hair is healthy, and you want to do all you can to keep it that way.

How to care for processed hair

When it comes to processed hair, adding moisture is the key – but there's one small problem here. Processed hair is often also combination hair, with oily roots but dry shafts and ends. And, just as with combination skin, tackling one leads to problems with the other. Washing processed hair is therefore a delicate balancing act of cleansing roots and moisturizing ends.

Let's deal with the cleansing first. If your hair is coloured, choose a shampoo that is specifically designed for coloured hair, as this means it will automatically be more gentle on your hair and will contain ingredients to preserve colour. If your hair is permed or relaxed, then choose any moisturizing shampoo, but in both cases make sure you apply it only to your roots and always rub it in well. Now apply a quick burst of water and, as the shampoo suds run down the hair shaft, gently massage the hair to remove any dirt and grime. Rinse well.

Once you have shampooed it is time to condition. Use a rich conditioner, primarily on the ends of the hair, smoothing the leftovers on your palms on the rest of the shaft. Rinse well – and that means *well*.

Processed hair is very porous and will drink in anything you put on it, making it harder for you to rinse out shampoos and conditioners. But the more layers of gunk there are between your hair and the light, the less shiny your hair will be. Make sure that the water in which you wash your hair is absolutely clear and then keep rinsing for one minute more before you put that showerhead away.

Dry your hair naturally whenever possible – heat can dehydrate hair further. Avoid harsh rubbing with a towel as this can make tangles in the hair and increase snapping of the strands. If you are using a blow-dryer, it's a good idea to first apply a little serum to the ends of the hair to seal in the moisture and so prevent further dehydration.

TOP 5 TIPS FOR PROCESSED HAIR

• Wash processed hair only every few days to prevent drying it out further. In between times use dry shampoo on the roots to absorb oil and grease.

• UV light adds to the problems of processed hair, stimulating oil production and drying out ends. Come summer, use UV-protectant hairsprays to screen out the rays.

• Don't assume a flaky scalp with processed hair means dandruff. It could be due to a shampoo that's too strong on the roots or, more likely, irritation due to the chemicals. If so, an anti-dandruff shampoo will only make things worse. Switch to a gentle shampoo instead. If things don't clear up within two weeks, then try the anti-dandruff approach.

• Use an intensive conditioning treatment on the ends of processed hair once a week. Try one with hot oil – or the recipe on page 81.

• Truly damaged hair can't be repaired and needs to be trimmed before the splits travel up the hair shaft, harming healthy hair. One sign of real damage is serious tangling when you comb the hair. This shows there are splits or tears in the hair shaft which is causing the hairs to web together. Book in for a trim – and ideally have everything cut from where those tangles start.

YOUR 5 KEY PRODUCTS
Colour preserving or
moisturizing shampoo
A rich conditioner
UV spray
Hot oil treatment
Serum

MAKE YOUR HAIR TREATMENT
For a rich mask that will restore essential nutrients to processed hair you should use a treatment that is based on dairy products. Mix the following ingredients together in a blender:

1 egg
1 oz cream cheese
1 oz cream
1 oz butter
1 oz water
¼ grapefruit

Apply the mixture to your hair and leave for at least five minutes. Rinse off in tepid water and leave to dry naturally if possible.

curly hair

What are the characteristics?

Curly hair is nearly always dry hair – this, combined with the fact that light reflects better from straight surfaces than curved ones, means that girls with curls often long for the sleek, shiny hair that they feel they will never have.

Curls also have a tendency to tangle and this can result in breaking and splitting. As your hair is already quite fragile, a considerable amount of TLC is crucial if you want to keep this type of hair in the best condition possible.

All of this pales in comparison, however, with the ultimate trauma for curly-haired girls – the dreaded frizz. All it needs is a tiny bit of moisture in the air for your sleek curls to turn into tangled webs. But you don't need to suffer in silence.

How to care for curly hair

Now this may shock you. If you have curly hair, never, ever, ever wash it every day. It tends to dehydrate the hair and make it more frizzy and unmanageable. Instead let your hair pick up some natural oils to help keep it calm and under control. If you have to wash to feel clean, skip shampoo and just rinse with water, then apply conditioner. When you wash, technique is crucial – use moisturizing shampoos and leave-in conditioners to add hydrating ingredients. For the best results comb through with a wide-toothed comb (the only way you should comb curly hair). Twice a month use an intensive conditioner or hot oil treatment (or try the treatment on page 85). When drying, don't rub your hair with the towel. Instead squeeze the excess water into the towel. Apply an anti-frizz styling cream or serum to the hair while it's still wet and leave it to dry naturally, or at least use a dryer with a diffuser and only moderate heat. And never tip the head upside down – you're asking for frizz.

'All it needs is a tiny bit of moisture in the air for your sleek curls to turn into tangled webs'

TOP 5 TIPS FOR CURLY HAIR

- If you find your brush is always tangling in your hair, splash out on one made of boar's hair bristles, which don't stick.
- If you don't want to fork out for that, just use your fingers – they're better for curly hair than most brushes and you won't have to spend a penny.
- If your curls have gone flat overnight don't think you need to style again. Just tip your head upside down and massage the hair near your scalp in a circular motion. This generates volume at the roots and wakes up your look.
- To protect curly hair from further dehydration always stop blow-drying just before the ends are completely dry. It's in the last few minutes of drying that the final water leaves the strands, leading to dehydration and breaking.
- Curly heads often think they can only have long hair to look good. Not true. Layered, short styles which prevent the hair from spilling outwards work as well as long, heavy locks.

YOUR 5 KEY PRODUCTS

Moisturizing shampoo
Leave-in conditioner
Hot oil treatment
Diffuser
Boar's bristle brush

'Curly heads often

think they can only

have long hair to

look good. Not true'

MAKE YOUR HAIR TREATMENT

For a rich, moisturizing mask that will add gloss and sheen to curly hair combine the following ingredients:

½ cup olive oil
10 drops lavender essential oil

Place the olive oil in a small saucepan and warm it gently (the oil should not be hot, just heated). Remove from the heat and add the lavender oil. Once you've double-checked the temperature, apply the mixture to your hair. Wrap it in a towel to maximize oil penetration and relax for 20 minutes. Wash out the oil with a gentle shampoo (you may need to repeat two or three times) and condition well.

wavy hair

What are the characteristics?

Hairdressers love wavy hair – it's often thick and coarse and there's normally loads of it to play with. It also suits both long and short styles easily. The trouble is, those of us who are blessed with wavy hair would rather it was either poker-straight or in tumbling ringlets – the grass is always greener! But why waste time wanting what you don't have when what you do have can look so fantastic?

The key to bringing out the beauty of wavy hair is dealing successfully with the two problems that come with it. The first of these is static, which can create the dreaded frizz, particularly on the crown of the head. The second is lack of volume, which can cause flattening at the roots, creating a bell-head look.

How to care for wavy hair

Thick, coarse hair can handle frequent washing but responds best to being left for two to three days between shampoos. When you do shampoo, you're unlikely to need thickening shampoos, but this doesn't mean that you should just grab any old bottle off the shelf. Because wavy hair is so thick, it can easily be weighed down, so using a volumizing shampoo (which provides lift within the hair) will counteract this and will help maximize bounce and life. Wash your hair and follow up with a light leave-in conditioner, which will provide a protective layer between the hair cuticle and the moisture that can create frizz.

Now it's time for drying, which is where you can create truly wonderful waves. Start by towel-drying the hair lightly (by pressing and patting, not rubbing, which again creates frizz).

For ultimate results, use the following wave-enhancing technique:

• Apply some anti-frizz serum or styling cream.
• Divide the hair into sections about one inch across.
• Using your fingers, twist these into ropes and fasten them up into little pin curls on your head.
• Leave to dry naturally.
• When the sections are dry, unravel and rake through with your fingers.

If you're in a hurry this approach won't work, so you're going to have to fake waves and volume. To do this, apply a little mousse to the roots of your hair, and blow-dry using a warm setting (hot will straighten the hair out) and pointing the dryer upwards. When hair is about 90 per cent dry, tip your head upside down and blow-dry that way.

TOP 5 TIPS FOR WAVY HAIR

• Before brushing, spray your brush with hairspray to prevent static.
• If you're caught with frizz, smoothing a tumble-dryer sheet over your locks will smooth things down.
• If you have short hair, waves can create unwanted height at the crown. The key to beating this is to know your flat zone. Waves within the hair start two or three inches down the hair shaft and once your hair reaches that length it will start to do stuff you just don't want. Know how long between cuts it takes for your hair to reach 'danger length' and book appointments accordingly.
• Go for regular trims, even if you have long hair. Split ends will create a fuzzball at the ends of your hair which destroys the look.
• Wavy hair won't reflect light like straight hair does, so it can often look dull. Make sure that you keep it moisturized – this will keep it glossy. Our recipe on page 89 should do the trick.

YOUR 5 KEY PRODUCTS
Volumizing shampoo
Leave-in conditioner
Mousse
Hairspray for brushes
Shine serum

'The key to bringing out

the beauty of wavy hair is

dealing successfully with

static and lack of volume'

MAKE YOUR HAIR TREATMENT

That slight kink in wavy hair can be enough to reduce the gloss on your hair. Intense moisturizing will help. For a shine-boosting mask that will help your hair recover its natural sheen use this fruit-based mask. Mash together the following ingredients in a large bowl:

½ ripe banana
½ avocado
1 heaped tsp plain yoghurt
1 tbsp olive oil

Apply the mixture to the hair, focusing on the ends and up to where the waves of your hair begin. This will moisturize these areas (which is where you want the shine) but won't weigh down the roots. Wrap your hair in a towel and relax for 20 minutes before rinsing.

straight hair

What are the characteristics?

Straight hair is normally fine and thin. This may surprise you, as everyone has seen those girls with manes of cascading, dead straight locks that look so thick you could knit blankets from them. Well, those girls just happen to have a lot of strands of fine hair. The result of this is that although straight hair looks fantastic in long straight styles or in short crops, if you want hair with body and bounce it's going to take some work to make those fine thin strands stand up and dance. This is particularly true if you are one of those Swedish blondes, as blonde hair is generally thinner than brunette or black hair (particularly that of Asians and Indians). This means the style that many of us see as the epitome of hair beauty — you know, that Goldilocks look — is probably the hardest to look after. Also because straight hair sits close to the head it often becomes greasy quickly at the roots and the fine strands absorb this rapidly, meaning you probably have to wash your hair every day.

How to care for straight hair

For that very reason, the most important thing straight hair needs is a gentle shampoo. Choose one that's marked for daily or frequent washing as it's likely to be low in detergents and high in moisturizers. Or at the very least use opaque shampoo — this tends to include more conditioners and so is kinder to the hair. Using moisturizing shampoo also means you may be able to get away without conditioner, which is the kiss of death to fine, straight hair as it weighs it down further. If you do want to use conditioning products make sure they are light (sprays are better than creams) and that you wash them out well. Never use leave-in or two-in-one products. If you want to create some bounce and body in your hair, thickening shampoos are your best friends. These normally include an ingredient called panthenol, which penetrates the hair cuticle, making each strand thicken; plus, they 'negatively charge' the hair so the strands are less likely to stick together — clever, eh?

When it comes to drying, your technique depends on the effect you want to create. For sleek looks, dry hair with a dryer with a nozzle. To create volume, use mousse or thickening gel on the roots of your hair and dry against your natural parting for the majority of the session, tipping your head upside down for the last two to three minutes.

'Using moisturizing shampoo also means you may be able to get away without conditioner, which is the kiss of death to fine, straight hair'

TOP 5 TIPS FOR STRAIGHT HAIR

• Your perfect brush is a flat paddle brush with wide bristles that separate the hair without damage.

• Avoid products with alcohol in their top three ingredients. Alcohol is great at helping tame thick, wavy hair but will make fine, straight strands cling together.

• Straight hair is the shiniest as light reflects from the cuticle. To maximize your natural asset, make the last rinse a cold one as this flattens the cuticle. Also, do the last two to three minutes of your blow-dry on the cool setting with the nozzle facing downwards. Shine serums will also help.

• If you're aiming for volume, try not to handle your hair too much. Heat and oil from your palms can be enough to make fine hair floppy.

• You can also add volume to your hair using colour. Mix highlights and lowlights in three or four different shades to create depth and texture.

YOUR 5 KEY PRODUCTS
Frequent wash or
thickening shampoo
Spray conditioner
Mousse or thickening gel
Shine serum
Paddle brush

MAKE YOUR
HAIR TREATMENT
Help cut oil production in your hair
with this oil-reducing astringent hair
rinse. Use the following ingredients:

I large jug of peppermint
tea (use two teabags)
Tea tree oil

Make up the peppermint tea and
leave it to cool. Add 10 drops of
tea tree oil. Pour over the head as a
final rinse.

face shapes

Recognizing your face shape is the key to choosing a cut and style that flatter you.

Choosing the right cut

To identify your face shape, scrape your hair back and look in the mirror at the proportions of your face and its angles. Compare what you see with the shapes on page 95.

What to look for

While the shape of your face is the starting point of your hairstyle, there are other things you need to consider.

• **Body build:** Your hair needs to balance this. For instance, if you're tall and big-boned, you'll need hair to balance your physique so skip short crops.

• **Your lifestyle:** If you want hair you can style in five minutes, don't go for a sleek bob. Choose tousled or layered styles which you can literally wash and go.

• **Your natural hair:** Wash your hair the day of a cut so the hairdresser can see how your hair works before it gets wet.

• **Glasses:** Glasses can alter your whole appearance. Even if you wear contact lenses, if you know you'll be wearing your glasses at some point make sure you take them along to show your stylist.

At the hairdresser's

The first step is finding someone you get on with. You need to feel you can communicate freely with your hairdresser.

• **Visit the salon:** Check out the age, style and hairdos of the clients and the staff. Does what you want fit in with their approach and image?

• **Take a picture with you:** This can work well so long as what you aspire to is realistic for your hair length and texture. Use pictures as your guide but make sure you ask the stylist to explain what elements of that look will work for you.

• **Think about care and maintenance:** Ask the stylist's advice on what products you will need to keep the style you're after in good shape. Then think about whether you are willing to blow-dry and use other products.

• **Don't be bullied:** Stick to your guns and keep your goal in mind. A sulky stylist is a bad stylist. And if they wash your hair before they've examined it and you've made your decision, leave – hair has to be seen dry if it is to be cut well.

Squoval

• **What are the characteristics?**

You have a wide, open forehead that's quite high. The sides of your face are flat, leading to a square or angled chin.

• **What suits you:** Anything that softens the angles of your face. Choose styles with soft wispy layers, waves or curls. The best looks for you are those with volume or curls at the crown of your head and sleek sides. Side partings will suit you better than centre ones, and you should always avoid blunt cut fringes.

Round

• **What are the characteristics?**

Your face is of pretty much uniform width all over. Your cheeks are also full.

• **What suits you:** Your aim is to slim and elongate your face, so avoid styles that end at your jawline as these round off your face further. Go for long styles – straight styles or those with choppy layers are best. If you go short, get sides that are cut onto the face rather than cropped sides. Finally, centre partings make the face rounder, so choose a wispy fringe or a long straight side parting instead.

Heart

• **What are the characteristics?**

Your forehead is wider than the lower half of your face, your chin is tapered or thin, and your cheeks are often full.

• **What suits you:** Balance is the key, so styles that are wider at the bottom than the top are best for you – flicked-out bobs work particularly well. Choose styles with a fringe, particularly one that sweeps over one side of the face – this breaks up the forehead and elongates the face.

Long

• **What are the characteristics?**

Long faces are often thin and most of the length is concentrated in the lower half of the face. Angles are pointed.

• **What suits you:** Your aim is to add width to the lower half of your face, so choose looks that are layered from the level of your top lip down. Or try the chin-length bob, which was made for your face shape. You can wear hair up, but only if the distance between your earlobe and the start of your chin is less than two inches. Otherwise the style will elongate your face and you'll look drawn.

hair colouring

Colour can be used to enhance – or completely change – your natural hair shade, but it's vital to choose the right colour, and the correct process to achieve that look.

Choosing your colour

Hair and skin are coloured by the same substance – melanin. That's why the colour of your hair generally matches your skin tone. Those with dark olive skins have dark brown hair, while white blondes have very pale skin. Finding a colour that suits you has to reflect this. The simplest way to avoid mistakes is to choose a colour no more than two shades lighter or darker than yours – it will always suit you. If you're using highlights (lighter streaks in the hair) or lowlights (darker streaks) you can go up to four shades different with no consequences.

If you are totally changing your colour, however, you have to pick your shade carefully. The wrong one can age you by years, make you look pale and washed out, or cause your features to vanish even with a truckload of make-up. Like make-up, your choice should be made on whether you have cool or warm tones in your skin. Cool-toned skins need ashy or 'light' blonde and brunette shades and bluey blacks; warm skins need shades based on coppers or reds (strawberry blonde, for example) and brown blacks rather than true blacks. And remember the shade on the box is normally what you get if you put the colour on white hair – what will happen on yours could be very different.

Choosing your colouring type

Whether you want an all-over colour that will be gone by morning or subtle lights that'll last for months, there's a colour process for you. But success relies on choosing the right one.

Temporary colours: Also known as wash-in, wash-out colours, they are water-based and lightly coat the hair shaft with colour. They last until the next wash. While wash-in colours are great to try out a new look, they do come with a couple of caveats. If you have highlights or bleach on your hair, be warned – they will stick to this longer than to your natural hair, leaving you with some very strange streaks when you wash out. Also, colours will wash out if it rains too heavily, and may rub off on pillows or white outfits.

Semi-permanent colours: These coat the outer hair shaft and penetrate the top layer of the cuticle, creating a colour that will wash out after four to six washes. Semi-permanents are best for those not completely committed to hair colour, but be warned, this convenience also means they will fade quickly if not protected from UV rays or bleaching agents like chlorine. To make the colour last longer, avoid washing your hair for two to three days after the initial application. If you have the opposite problem and can't stand the colour, washing-up liquid will strip the colour. Just make sure you condition well afterwards.

Tone-on-tone colours: Between semi-permanent and permanent colours, these use low levels of peroxide to help the colour penetrate the hair shaft, but wash out rather than grow out after five to twelve weeks. Because semi-permanent colours contain no bleach, you'll find that they don't always work well if you're trying to lighten dark hair. This is where tone-on-tone colours really come into their own, as they lighten without the commitment (and roots) that come with permanent colours. Care advice is the same as for semi-permanent colours, but the washing-up liquid trick won't work very well.

Permanent colours: These colours use ammonia or other chemicals that open the hair shaft and allow the colour to penetrate into the cuticle, staining it permanently. The colour will last until it naturally grows out, though poor maintenance may cause the colour to fade and you'll lose the glossy sheen that makes tinted hair look so good. Always wash with shampoos made for coloured hair. Finally, when your roots come through, colour them alone. Applying permanent colour to the whole head

over and over again is the fastest way to break hair.

Henna: An extract of the henna plant, this uses an ingredient called lawsone to coat the hair shaft. Henna is one of the most misunderstood colorants, as everyone thinks it's natural and therefore good for the hair. In fact this is not true – henna can coat the hair so thickly that it actually stops conditioners from penetrating the hair, creating a dry, frizzy mess. With so many good colorants out there now, messing around with henna really isn't worthwhile. It's a permanent hair colour and no other colour should be used with it.

Highlights: These use bleaching agents to lighten the hair. Most home kits use caps with tiny holes in that the hair is pulled through, creating thin streaks. In salons, most colourists paint the colour on strips of hair which creates a more natural look. For best results choose a kit offering this approach. They are permanent but root regrowth isn't as noticeable as with permanents. Since they use bleach, they are one of the harshest home procedures – and the one most likely to go wrong. Never try and highlight dark brown or black hair at home – it will just go orange. If you are looking for lighter streaks, seek out professional help. If you are suitable for home highlights, increase your chances of success by never leaving the colour on longer than directed, because your hair will snap. Neither should you take it off before it's done – you'll get brassy stripes, not sun-kissed streaks.

Lowlights: These are strips of usually permanent colour applied throughout the hair that are darker than your natural colour, to create depth. Getting the right shade for lowlights is trickier than it looks; choose wrong and your hair will look dull. It's a good idea to get lowlights done professionally if you can.

Colours for grey hair: These work in the same way as permanent or semi-permanent colours but the pigment is adapted for grey hair. They last from four weeks to forever, depending on which you use. If you have more than 50 per cent grey, these specialist colorants are essential – the lack of pigment in grey hair alters the shade of 'normal' colorants so that browns can go green and blondes can go pink! When choosing a shade to cover grey hair, aim for one a few shades lighter than your original colour. Our skin tone changes as we age and your natural colour could now be too dark for your skin.

Correct application

If you're applying an all-over tint (semi or permanent), correct application is the final step to looking good.

But first, it's important that you make sure your skin isn't allergic to the colouring product. Twenty-four hours before you colour, patch-test it on the skin behind your ear. Five in every 100 people are allergic to some types of hair-dye, and if you're one of them it is much better to find out on the space behind your ear than across your entire scalp.

On the day itself, wash your hair before you colour, as product build-up on the hair can prevent colour taking – or even change the colour. Apply Vaseline around your hairline to stop colour running and staining the skin. Never apply colour to the top of the head and then rub it in – you'll get patches. Instead, divide the hair into four or five sections and treat each individually. Apply a strip of colour to the root and massage it down the hair shaft.

Leave the colour in exactly as long as directed before rinsing well. Make sure you check for misplaced colour – it can stain your ears, the back of your neck and around the hairline. If you do find any, an alcohol-based skin cleanser will remove it. Or you could try this hairdressers' trick:: mix cold cigarette ash with a little water to make a paste, then rub into the skin for 1-2 minutes. Wash it off with water.

the hairstyling equipment kit

While a professional cut should ensure your hair keeps on looking good day to day, maintaining healthy, shining hair takes the right equipment. And sometimes you just want to liven things up. This kit will help you do both.

Blow-dryer

The best blow-dryers are between 1,400 and 1,600 watts. This will speed drying time, reducing the hair's exposure to heat. They should also have a diffuser and a nozzle so you can direct the air.

Clockwise from top: Blow-dryer attachments (nozzle and diffuser); mini-paddle brush; teasing comb; styling comb; round brush; flat-backed brush.

Round brush

The best brush to use while styling hair as it allows you to move through the hair while you blow-dry.

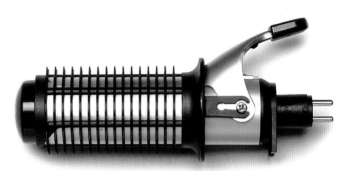

Tongs

Good for creating precise, ringlety curls or flicky styles.

Straightening irons

For adding shine to hair and taming waves or curls.

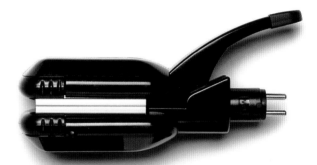

Butterfly clips

Essential to separate off sections of your hair while you style.

Rollers

Large rollers can help give volume to hair.

Setting lotions or styling waters

These are spritzed onto the hair to create hold while you're styling.

From the top:
Curling tong; curling tong attachment for bigger curls or waves; straightening iron attachment; velcro rollers.

Mousse

Used to create body in styles. For best results apply a golfball-sized blob mainly to the roots of the hair to give lift.

Gel

For more sculpted, defined styles, it gives more lasting hold than mousse. Too much will make hair stiff though, so use a pea-sized blob on short styles or a 10p-sized blob on long styles.

Wax

For tousled or messy styles that need control and shine, use wax. It's better on short hair than long and always remember that using too much will make hair sticky and attract dirt. For best results, use a pearl-sized blob warmed in your palms and smoothed down the hair – wipe off any excess.

Serum

Used to create shine, it doesn't really hold hair in place but just enhances the finished result. Use no more than a pea-sized blob of serum on short styles, a 10p-sized one on long – more than that will make your hair look greasy.

Hairspray

The finishing touch. Don't spray it directly onto your hair, as this will make it stiff. Instead spray a fine mist over the hair from about four inches away. This will set without stickiness or stiffness.

Hair elastics

The only way to put hair up, they are smooth to the touch and don't snag.

From left: hair wax; mousse; gel.

Clockwise from top left: butterfly clips; hair combs; hair slides; barette; mini-butterfly clips; hairgrips; barette; styling clips; hair slides.

ponytail

The ponytail is often thought of as a casual kind of style, but if perfect it can see you happily through from dawn to dusk.

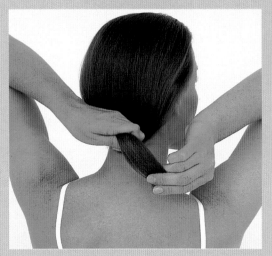

1 Wash and dry your hair. You will need clean locks, otherwise oil from the roots will be combed down the hair shaft, making the ponytail look lank. Apply a little shine serum from root to tip to keep frizzy ends under control and create a glossy 'tail'.

2 Lean your head back and brush all your hair off your face and up towards the top of your head. If you can do this lying over the edge of the bed you'll get an even better result.

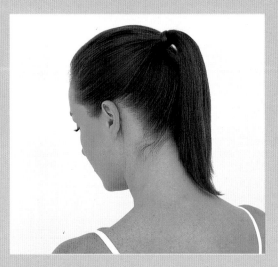

3 Leave one small section loose and secure the rest with a tight covered band. Wrap the loose section of hair around the band.

4 Secure the end of the loose section with a hair grip on the underside of the ponytail.
The result will be a sophisticated, sleek finish.

ponytail variations

It can also be fun to experiment with this simple style. Whether for work or for play, use accessories to adapt your ponytail to any occassion.

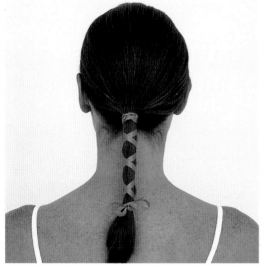

Ribbon ponytail
Secure your ponytail at the nape of your neck. Wrap a length of ½ inch ribbon round the top so you are left with two ends, then criss-cross these down the tail. Secure at the bottom with a neat bow.

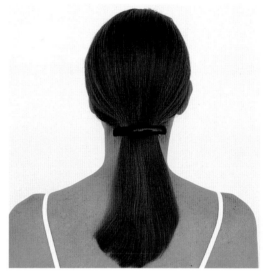

Work ponytail
A barette will finish off a low ponytail perfectly, creating a more sophisticated look. Secure your ponytail at the nape of the neck.

Party ponytail
Beaded bracelets make perfect hair decorations – wear as many as you dare.

two looks in one

Achieve these two fun and funky styles quickly and with minimum effort. Perfect for before and after a party, they will work best with chin- to shoulder-length hair.

1 For an easy-to-achieve party look, divide your hair into seven equal sections. Apply hairspray to one section, twist, then twirl it into a knot. Fasten with a hairgrip. Repeat this around your whole head.

2 Remove the hairgrips and shake out your hair. This simple undo will leave masses of springy curls.

EASY HAIR TIPS

You can jazz up both of these looks using jewelled accessories. Follow the directions for the first, but fasten each knot with a hairgrip which has diamanté glued to its end. Your funky party hairdo will sparkle all night long.

Then, when you shake out your curls, fasten back any hair falling over your face with one or two of the diamanté hairgrips. Your hair will maintain the wildness of the curls but it will look slightly tamed.

french twist

This simple style looks elegant – and terribly complicated to anyone who sees it.
If only they knew how easy it was!

1 | Brush your hair over to one side of your head.

2 Now, gripping your hair in one hand, bring it up towards the crown of your head, twisting as you do this to create a tight roll. When you reach the top, use a few pins to secure the ends in place.

3 Use a tail comb to pull a few strands of hair loose around your face or by your ears.

sleek shiny hair

This straight look can be done on any hair type – yes, even the curliest of hair – although we warn you, this is not a job for the faint-hearted or those in a rush.

1 Hair should be wet to allow the blow-dryer heat to reset the hair.

2 Now spray with setting lotion and comb this through so every strand is lightly coated.

3 Separate your hair into four or five sections. Use a round brush to comb down the first section of hair, pulling it straight. Blow-dry this using the hot setting on your dryer. To avoid burning the hair, keep the dryer moving and keep brushing the hair until dry.

4 By now your hair should be dry and about 90 per cent straight. Apply a little shine serum to coat (but not dampen) the hair, then use straightening irons to smooth out those last little kinks.

5 The end result is fabulously sleek locks. If you do have curly hair, bear in mind that to blow-dry it straight takes about an hour – and you could really do with an extra set of hands. Now all you have to do is pray it doesn't rain!

full and wavy

To create sexy waves with lots of volume you'll need some old-fashioned setting techniques combined with new haircare technology.

1 Wash your hair with a volumizing shampoo and conditioner – these products will swell the hair shaft, so creating thicker hair.

2 Apply a tennisball-sized blob of volumizing mousse to the hair, combing it through so that each strand is coated. Dry the hair but not completely – it should be about 80 per cent dry.

3 While the hair is still hot from the hair-dryer, divide it in eight to ten sections and wind around large rollers. Continue to blow-dry until it is completely dry.

4 Remove the rollers but don't brush. Instead, tip your head upside down and spritz a little volumizing hairspray through the roots.

5 Shake the look out with your fingers. Again, don't
brush, as that will flatten.

fun funky crown braids

Black hair can have beautiful curls, but they're often too hard to handle. Let your natural beauty shine through with this fun look.

1 Clip the hair from the top of your head up and out of the way. You need to work on the sides first.

2 Take a piece of hair at ear level and comb it straight. Now, plait the hair (take the right over the centre, then the left and repeat). As you do this pull the plait towards the back of your head.

EASY HAIR TIPS

This also looks great if you stop the plaits half-way down. Put on an alice band or a bright headscarf to hide the elastics, then fluff out the rest of your curls.

Bear in mind that some people have difficulty doing these braids by themselves. To make your work faster and easier, ask a friend to help you out.

3 When you get to the bottom of the plait, secure with a small hair elastic. Repeat this across your head.

cascading curls

This look works best on curly or naturally wavy hair. While you can ringlet dead straight hair, it takes a lot of expertise.

1 Wash your hair the day before your special night out. Some styles work best on hair that's got a little natural oil in it – and this is one of them. Now lightly spritz the hair with setting lotion; it should be damp, not wet.

2 Take a section of hair about one inch wide and wrap this sideways around a hot curling iron. Hold for 10 seconds.

3 Remove the iron, but don't brush out the ringlet yet. Instead, coil it back up and secure it to your head with a hairclip. Repeat this around your whole head and leave for 10 minutes.

4 Gently unwind the curls and comb them through with your fingers.

eat your way to better hair

As with skin, what you eat affects your hair. Hair follicles rely on nourishment from the bloodstream, but they compete with the rest of your body for nutrients.

In the body's pecking order, hair is a non-essential organ. If your diet is lacking, nutrients are diverted to higher-priority organs, and your hair misses out. The result is hair that's dry and slow to grow.

Beating this is simple – just make sure you eat a well-balanced diet rich in fruit and vegetables, with at least two servings of protein a day and large amounts of energy-giving wholegrain carbohydrates. This will ensure optimum nutrition for the entire body and your hair will get its fair share. It'll then grow at its maximum speed (normally around 14mm a month), strength and thickness.

You can also help prevent particular hair problems with diet. This doesn't mean that a good breakfast will beat a bad hair day – hair takes three months to grow, so that's how long it will take to see the results of any dietary changes. Nor can you eat your way out of a bad hairdo. No amount of vitamins will repair hair that's chemically damaged or split. But you can help some other things.

Oily hair

While naturally oily hair is genetically determined (and nothing you eat can beat your genes), if your hair has suddenly turned oily, check your spice intake. Foods that cause the skin to sweat like curries or chilli also cause the scalp to sweat and this increases oil levels.

Dull hair

Lack of shine in your hair means that it's not reflecting the light properly. Healthy hair is formed with a flat cuticle, and when light rays hit this they bounce back. That's what creates the shine. However, if the cuticle on the hair lifts, that reflection won't happen and hair will look dull. So why does the cuticle lift? While chemical processes like bleaching are the most common cause, lack of protein also causes the hair to grow with a lifted cuticle. It is recommended that you eat 0.75g of protein (like lean meat, poultry, fish, dairy products, nuts, seeds or pulses) per kilogram of body weight a day.

Dry hair

This is one of the common symptoms of essential fatty acid deficiency. This is particularly true if your hair is flyaway and frizzy. Boost EFAs by eating nuts, seeds and oily fish like mackerel. These foods also supply protein, which is vital for glossy hair; without it, the hair forms with a lifted cuticle which reduces the hair's natural protection, making it easier for moisture to evaporate and drying to occur.

Hair that won't grow

The B vitamins, which provide the body with energy, are vital for hair growth. If your energy levels are low, hair growth slows down. Eating little and often will help to keep energy levels up. Biotin (sometimes called vitamin H) also helps create thicker, faster-growing hair. You'll find it in eggs, fish, milk, nuts and pulses.

Thinning hair

This tends to be linked to iron deficiency. Ensure you're reaching around 14.8mg of iron a day from a supplement or by filling your diet with lean red meat or dark green vegetables. Also, too much vitamin A (over 10,000 units a day) can lead to hair loss. This is only likely to happen if you are taking in high levels of A-heavy foods or if you're mixing supplements. If you are, stop. Vitamin A is toxic to the body and hair loss is the first sign of this. If you want extra vitamin A for your skin, increase your intake of fruit and vegetables.

HAIR Q&A

Let us help you with your most common haircare questions.

Q: I'm convinced I'm losing my hair. How much fall-out is too much?
A: The average person loses 100 hairs a day, so anything less than that really isn't a problem. Also, hair fall-out tends to be greater in October and November, as this is when the hair reaches maturity in its growth cycle. In fact, you should only really be concerned about the amount of hair you are losing if you can see your scalp through your hair. If this happens see a trichologist (an expert in hair problems). Many things can cause hair loss, from poor nutrition to overly tight ponytails, and a trichologist will be able to help diagnose and offer any appropriate treatment.

Q: Can my hair 'get used' to its shampoo, making it less effective?
A: No, it's not true that if you use the same products regularly they become less effective. If you like a shampoo and it's right for your hair, stick with it. The only reason to change would be if your hair type changes, which can happen with age, if you chemically treat your hair, or when the seasons change – heat makes hair get oilier, whereas cold dries it out.

Q: Is it a myth that you should brush your hair 100 times a day?
A: Yes. This can actually damage the root and tear the hair shaft. Just brush two or three times to get the tangles out. Start at the ends of the hair, holding the strands about half-way up to prevent tugging at the root, and work out any knots carefully to prevent splitting.

Q: I have split ends. Can I mend them?
A: This one's a common question – and a quick one to answer. No. Nothing can mend a split end, though serums will temporarily seal them, making your hair look less bitty. The only way to treat a split end is to snip it off – and you should do it before it splits up the hair shaft, damaging your hair further.

Q: How can I tell if I have dandruff?

A: Dandruff occurs when a bacteria causes skin cells to clump on the scalp. These are usually white or grey in appearance and flake off easily. The problem is that this is easily confused with two other conditions. Let's deal with the easy one first. Dandruff is not greasy – if the scalp and scales are greasy you've another problem called seborrhoeic dermatitis, which should be treated with cortisone creams. The other problem is a dry scalp, which is harder to distinguish from dandruff. This is normally caused by shampoos that are too harsh, so the best way to find out if it's dandruff or a dry scalp is to switch to a gentle shampoo and some intensive conditioning. If things don't get better after three or four washes, it's dandruff and you should treat it with a specialist shampoo.

Q: Can I perm and colour my hair at the same time?

A: Not at home. The chemicals can easily interact and lead to breaking. A professional hairdresser can do both, so ask their advice about what should be done when. Tell your hairdresser everything you've used on your hair – any chemical could upset the process and cause damage. The thing most people forget is henna, which, despite its natural image, often contains chemicals.

Q: I coloured my hair and it's snapped. Now what?

A: Well, nothing will repair the hair – you just need to make it look better. You can do this by having the most damaged areas cut by a good hairdresser and by flooding the rest with moisture via intensive conditioning treatments. Other than that, you'll just have to wait for healthier hair to grow back in its place. You can speed growth by massaging the scalp daily – particularly with products containing menthol, which stimulates blood flow to the scalp.

4

make-up

Make-up can work miracles – just look at celebrities. On screen they look perfect, with wide eyes and lush full lips, but in those sneaky paparazzi shots they look just like the rest of us. Their perfection is down to make-up – and soon yours can be too. We've already looked at how the right colours can help flatter your skin tone. Now we're about to see how tricks and tips of application can help make the most of your features. If you want wider, brighter eyes, we'll show you how to get them; fuller, sexier lips, it's all down to the lipstick you choose. And by learning how to create the perfect base for your colours, you need never look tired or stressed out again. You can even change your whole image in the blink of an eye – from sexy party looks to girly pinks, the choice is yours. You just need to know how to make it happen.

Creating a perfect base is the most important step in make-up. Without it your eye and lip shades will highlight imperfections such as lines, spots or redness. Base make-up to most people means a mask of foundation, but that's not necessarily the case at all. If you've got great skin, then all a base need mean to you is a dab of well-applied concealer and some blusher. However, most of us do need a little more coverage than that – or maybe you prefer the groomed feeling that a full base offers. In this case it's vital to ensure you're choosing the right products for your needs, in the right colour for your skin tone. And that's where many of us slip up – or have done until now, that is.

foundation and powder equipment kit

If you're applying a full base, foundation and powders are the products to choose. Here's what's out there, and what they do.

Liquid foundation

Creates sheer to medium coverage. It can be applied with a sponge, but many make-up artists prefer to use their fingers as they claim the warmth helps it blend better. Use it sparingly – too much will look like a mask.

Stick foundation

Offers more coverage and is faster to blend than liquid. It should only ever be blended with the fingers or it can go streaky. It's good if you have small blemishes or eye circles and don't want to use concealer.

Cream-to-powder foundation

If you like the look of a matt face, choose these. Applied with a damp sponge they create a dewy, matt finish that gives full coverage.

Tinted moisturizer

The lightest coverage, this is the product for you if you don't like foundation. Many women think it makes you look tanned. It shouldn't – like foundation, it should match your skin.

Bronzing gels/sticks

If you want a more sun-kissed look, bronzing gel is the product for you – but choose sheer brands and apply sparingly. You're trying to enhance your natural colour, not create a fake tan.

Left:: Pressed powder
Right: loose powder with puff;
sponge wedges; pressed powder.

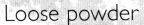

Loose powder

Used to set foundation, it should be brushed lightly over the face with a big fluffy brush. Translucent is the best shade to choose, but if you have warm skin choose one that's yellow-based rather than pink.

Pressed powder

To create total coverage, apply over foundation. However, don't smooth it on the skin; apply it with a powder sponge in a rolling motion.

Bronzing powder or spheres

Brushed lightly across the skin, this creates a golden glow. However, don't use it all over the face, as this will make the skin look dirty rather than tanned. Instead, only apply it where the sun naturally hits your skin – the cheekbones, chin and tip of your nose.

Foundation sponge

It's not essential but many women prefer it to fingers. Wash the sponge after every use in a little baby shampoo.

Powder brush

Essential for applying loose powder, the perfect brush is roughly three centimetres across and fluffy. Again, wash it regularly with baby shampoo.

what it all means

Confused by the terms on your products? Here's how to break through the lingo.

FIRMING:
These use ingredients that tighten the skin while you wear them. They minimize fine lines and wrinkles. Good for maturing skins.

LIGHT-REFLECTIVE:
As we get older the skin reflects less light, so to counteract this some products add light-reflective particles. They give the face a glow and create the illusion of fewer lines and wrinkles. They're good for maturing skin or those who feel their skin looks dull.

MOISTURIZING:
These include ingredients that hydrate the skin while you wear them. Best for dry or mature skins.

OIL-FREE:
Oily ingredients have been taken out to minimize shine.

PLUMPING:
The latest trend in foundation is to include ingredients that 'plump' the skin as you wear them, reducing the look of lines and wrinkles. Good for anyone worried about ageing.

SUN PROTECTION FACTOR (SPF):
Includes sunscreen, but don't rely on it – foundation is spread so thinly, it won't give the same protection as a moisturizer or specialist sunscreen.

TREATMENT FOUNDATION:
These normally contain salicylic acid to help counteract spots while you are wearing them.

VITAMIN-ENRICHED:
Enhanced with antioxidants, these claim to give more defence against problems like pollution.

TOP 5 TIPS FOR USING FOUNDATION

• Never test foundation on your hand – it's always a different colour from your face. Always apply it to your jawline. The right shade for you is the one that disappears into your skin.

• If you can't decide between two foundation shades choose the lighter one, as darker foundations create more obvious tidemarks. This advice changes for black skin, however. Matching foundation to the lightest areas of your face can make you look ashy. Match the darkest and you'll look overly made up. If you find it hard to find the right shade, go for one that matches your neck; this is normally a balance between the two.

• You're wearing too much foundation if you can't see any of the pores on your skin. Your natural texture is supposed to show through a little.

• If your make-up starts to shine, use blotting paper rather than reapplying powder, which can often start to look too heavy.

• For a softer look on a night out, apply your foundation before you have your bath (run it warm rather than boiling hot). The steam sets the foundation and creates a really dewy look.

applying a perfect base

Learning how to apply a foundation base properly is the key to your whole make-up look. Follow these steps for a smooth and flawless complexion.

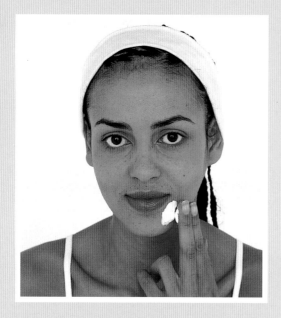 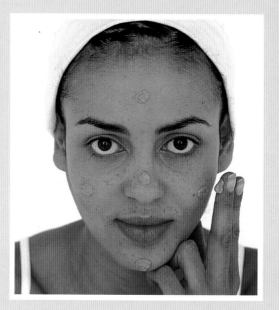

1 Apply moisturizer five minutes before you start your make-up. All bases will go on much more smoothly if your skin is well hydrated. Tissue off any excess – while hydrated skin is good for foundation, greasy skin will make it slip and slide.

2 Remember less is more, so don't apply big swathes; instead put a few dots around your face. Now, using your fingers or a foundation sponge, blend those dots together. Make sure you blend well around your hairline and jaw. If you've chosen the right shade there shouldn't be a join, but it's better to be safe than sorry.

3 Once the foundation has settled into the skin, check if there are any obvious under-eye shadows or blemishes
showing through. If there are, use concealer on these – we'll tell you exactly how in the next section. If you
want a matt finish, apply loose powder with a brush, or for heavier coverage press it into the skin with a soft puff.

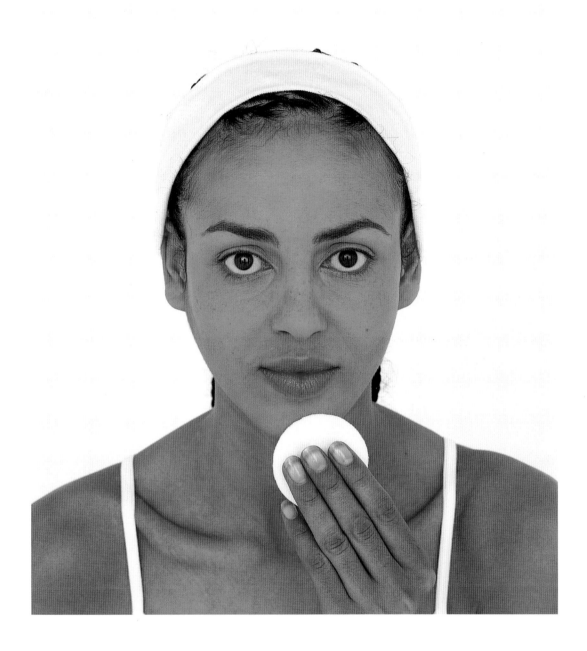

the concealer equipment kit

Concealer can be used either with foundation, to get rid of any last-minute imperfections, or alone, to just neaten your face. Here's what's out there.

Stick concealer

Normally found in light, medium or dark, these thick concealers are best for covering spots.

Wand concealer

More moisturizing than stick concealers, these are better for covering under-eye circles and evening out skin tone around the nose.

Medicated concealer

Very drying, these should only ever be used on spots – beware, they are often very pink.

Pencil concealer

Usually drier than liquid or stick concealers, they are great for covering spots and small blemishes.

Concealer brush

The best way to apply concealer of any type, it helps you mix shades.

Left: Stick concealers.
Right from top: concealer brush;
two concealer wands.

TOP 5 TIPS FOR USING CONCEALER

• Always apply concealer after foundation – until you have a base, you don't know exactly what you need to camouflage. What's more, applying foundation over concealer can easily rub it off. The concealer must be the same shade as your foundation – you may even have to buy two shades and mix them on your hand before you apply them. If you're using stick concealers, you may find that using a little eye cream will help mix the two shades together.

• If you're not wearing foundation, concealer must still match your skin tone. Using too light a shade on dark circles (as many women do) will actually make them more noticeable, and a light shade on a spot will highlight its shape.

• Never use a magnifying mirror when you apply concealer. It's tempting, but you'll put on too much.

• You've probably seen green concealers for sale. They claim to reduce redness. Avoid them, they are almost impossible to use without giving the skin a grey cast. If you have high colour, a foundation with yellow undertones will cancel out the redness just as well.

• If you're using your concealer to cover scars or to work on heavily pigmented blemishes like birthmarks, you will need a heavy concealer.

how to apply concealer

Nasty spots and dark circles under the eyes make your skin look tired and run down. Here's how to beat them.

Covering a spot

1 Don't pick the spot. Wet spots go crusty and can't be concealed. To reduce inflammation, apply a small amount of spot treatment containing benzoyl peroxide, salicylic acid, lavender or tea tree oil, leave to sink in, then blot any excess.

2 Apply concealer in the same shade as your foundation directly onto the spot (use a wand or a brush if you wish). Using your fingers, blend outwards from the centre. Do not just rub the concealer over the spot – this dilutes the coverage exactly where it's needed the most.

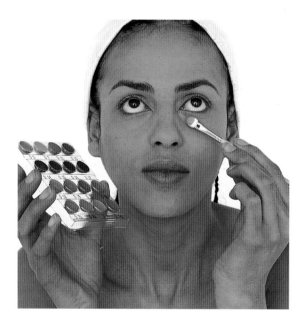

Covering under-eye bags

1 Use a concealer just one shade darker than your foundation. Apply to the puffy part of the bag – this will make it appear to recede.

2 Now take a lighter concealer and apply this in the crease at the base of the bag, blending well. This brings that part of the eye 'forward' and balances out the area. Powder over the whole thing.

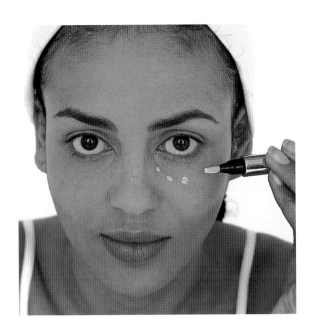

Covering under-eye circles

1 After you've applied foundation, get into bright or (preferably) natural light. Now tilt your chin down while looking into the mirror.

2 Apply three or four dots of concealer at the lower edge of the dark circle where it meets your cheek, starting these dots at the inside of your nose and moving to about three-quarters of the way along the eye.

3 Now use your middle finger to blend these dots upwards, outwards and downwards until the circle is covered. Keep coverage light at the outside corner of the eye, as anything heavy here will tend to accentuate lines and wrinkles.

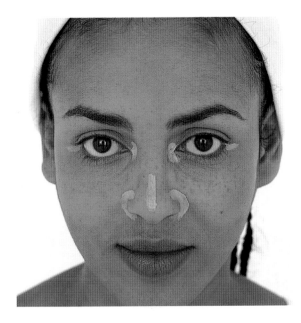

Using concealer instead of foundation

1 Moisturize the skin well. For this look to work, you have to have glowing skin underneath. Don't forget to use an eye cream on the eye area. This can be very dry and the skin won't absorb the concealer properly.

2 Cover up any spots as shown opposite. Now do the same with under-eye circles.

3 Finally, dab concealer on the nose and around the nostrils where most skin is red. Blend this well into the cheeks. Brush with loose powder. Now apply blusher.

the blusher equipment kit

The final step in creating the base of your look is blusher. Most women avoid it, but used correctly it can be the best beauty tool you own. Here's what's out there.

Powder blusher

The densest type, it's best applied after translucent powder as powder adheres best to powder. It's also the only one to use if you want to 'sculpt' your face with the blusher.

Cream blusher

Best applied with fingers, this offers dense colour but still lets your skin shine through. Apply it over foundation and before powder.

Gel blusher

If you want just a sheer glow, then this is the type of blusher you should go for. Apply it with your fingers either on bare skin or over foundation.

Tint blusher

Very sheer and long-lasting, but it dries fast and can look streaky over foundation. If you're going to use it, blend it fast and blend it well.

Shimmers

Once called highlighters, these were used as part of complicated face-sculpting regimes. Now they just give a light gleam to the top of your cheekbones. They're great for evening but normally unnecessary during the day.

Blusher brush

A round blusher brush is vital for natural effects. Avoid the flat sort that come in compacts – they create stripes.

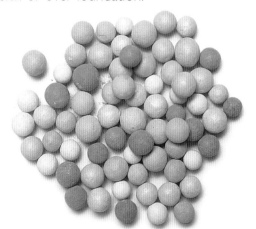

Left: blusher balls.
Right from top: powder blusher;
strip of gel blusher; strip of cream blusher;
bronzer balls; blusher brushes.

TOP 5 TIPS FOR USING BLUSHER

• The best way to work out where to put blusher is to go for a walk on a cold day. Where you flush is the most natural place for you to accentuate.

• If you're using powder blush, brush it on only one way – going over and over or round and round with the brush creates streaks.

• When using gel or tint blushes to contour the face, don't just apply one big blob and try to blend it. Chances are the colour will take more where it's first applied and you'll find it hard to even things out. Instead, apply a blob on the apple of the cheek and two smaller blobs graduating up the cheekbone, then blend upwards towards the hairline.

• Gel or tint blushes are best used on bare skin; they tend to stick on foundation and can be hard to blend.

• While the shade of blush you choose is generally determined by your skin tone, bear in mind that dusky pink blush can warm up any tired-looking skin.

how to apply blusher

There's no one correct way to apply blusher. The method you use depends on the type of look you want to create.

For a natural healthy glow

1 Apply foundation (and if necessary powder) as normal. Smile – where your cheek is naturally at its fattest is where blusher needs to go to create a natural look.

2 Apply the blusher in a small circle, blending well. For the best results, try gel blusher. Powder over the top.

For sexy cheekbones

1 Using powder blusher, sweep colour in an arc following the line of your cheekbone up from the apple of your cheek to your hairline. Keep colour light and blended – you want a wash rather than a stripe of colour.

2 Add a little shimmer on the highest point of your cheekbone nearest your eye.

EASY BLUSHER TIPS

It's important to keep your brushes clean, otherwise they'll gather bacteria and transfer it onto your skin. This will inevitably cause spots and blackheads.

An effective and quick way to clean your blusher brush is to use baby wipes. These will also clean any other make-up brushes you may have.

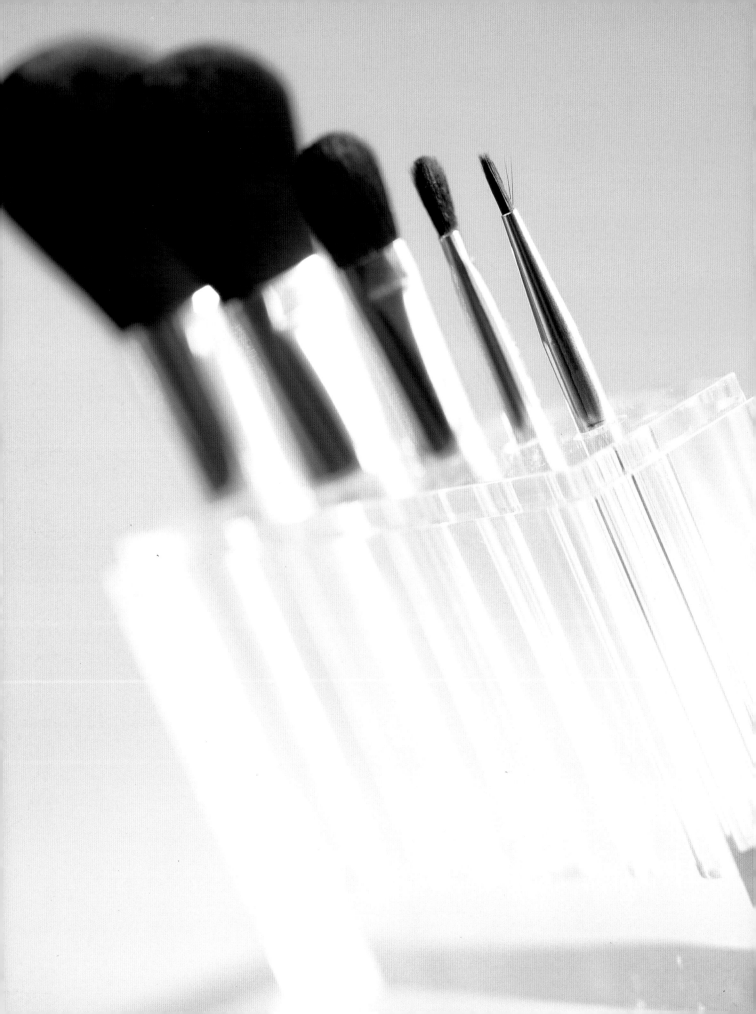

For a sun-kissed sheen

1 Using a blusher brush containing only a hint of bronze or pinky-brown powder, sweep colour along your cheekbone and then up round your hairline across your forehead. Again be careful that it doesn't look like a stripe, just a brush of colour. Repeat on the other side so the colour joins.

2 If you have gone too heavy with the bronzer, wipe the blusher brush clean and then use it to blend. This will soften the colour. Another trick which will help reduce the colour further, should you feel you need it, is adding a little translucent powder over the top. Be careful not to build up too much powder though, as this will just make your skin look caked with make-up.

BASE Q & A

Let us help you with your most common make-up base questions.

Q: My foundation always looks great in the shop, but orange when I apply it at home. Why?

A: This happens when oils on your skin interfere with ingredients in the foundation. You don't have to have oily skin for it to happen, nor will it occur with every brand. The best way to beat it when you're buying is to wait two to three minutes before checking a test patch in the mirror. Then find some natural light and choose the shade you can't see.

Q: I've just started wearing foundation and now I have acne. Did the make-up cause it?

A: No, the idea that foundation makes acne worse is a myth. Acne is caused by bacteria, not make-up. However, foundation could aggravate it if you're not cleaning it off properly at night, increasing the risk of pore blockage, or if you're not cleaning your sponges, reinfecting your skin the next time you use them. Wash them every night. Finally, if you are still worried, switch to foundations for acne-prone skin. These contain salicylic acid, which helps reduce bacteria on the skin while you use them.

Q: I have very dry skin and blusher always goes blotchy. What can I do?

A: This tends to happen if you apply blush direct to dry, bare skin. The skin sucks the oils out of the powder and leaves dusty, blotchy pigment on the surface. Beat it by wearing foundation or tinted moisturizer with a little powder over the top – or if you prefer the natural look, then just layer your blush. Smooth moisturizer over your skin, then apply a cream blush and finally powder over with your chosen shade. This will stop the blotching and make the colour last longer.

Q: I've seen products called colour-correctors in the shops. What do they do exactly?

A: The idea of colour-correctors is that some colours when used together cancel each other out – such as green concealer covering redness. Colour-correctors use this principle to fight sallowness in skin (a lilac corrector beats yellowness) or to brighten dull skin (by using a white corrector). You're supposed to add the corrector to your foundation. Like the green concealer, however, they are a lot easier to use badly than well. It's better to choose the right shade of foundation for your face and use your other make-up to enhance features.

Q: My concealer stings my eyes. Why?

A: You're applying it too close to the rim of the eye. When covering dark circles, the main focus of the colour should be where the circle meets the cheek. Blend upwards – this graduates colour and prevents it slipping into the eyes. If it still hurts, switch to a hypoallergenic product, from which the most common allergens will have been removed.

Q: I've never worn foundation before. Now I'm older I find I need it but hate wearing it. Is there a middle ground?

A: Yes. There's a trick make-up artists use, and that's to apply foundation only to the areas of your face that need extra coverage. These are normally the nose, chin, eyelids and brow bone. Obviously, you need to have exactly the right colour match, but if you use our tips to get the shade right for you and blend well around the joins, you'll have a few foundation-free years yet.

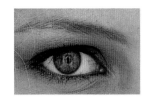

Our eyes are the first thing anyone notices about our face – and to give the right impression yours need to be bright, sparkling and attention-grabbing. The only problem is that using computers and going short of sleep can mean eyes are often red and puffy – grabbing attention for all the wrong reasons. Learning how to beat these problems is an important part of eyecare – but equally important is knowing how to make the most of your eyes with make-up. Every shadow you use on your face matters.

the eyecare equipment kit

Creating beautiful eyes means choosing the right types of product — here's what you will need.

Matt powder eyeshadows

Perfect for naturals and brights, matt powders suit everybody. For a deeper colour, apply them with a damp brush.

Shimmery shadows

These add glamour to eyes but are better suited to younger skin, as any specks falling into fine lines and wrinkles will highlight the problem.

Cream eyeshadows

Quick and easy to use, but can wear off quickly. Apply a little translucent powder underneath to help set them. Creams aren't ideal for older eyes as they may disappear into folds and lines.

Thickening mascaras

These plump out the lashes from root to tip, creating a wider looking lash.

Lengthening mascaras

These work by adding fibres to the tips of the lashes, making them longer.

Curling mascaras

These shrink on the lashes, giving them a natural curl.

Waterproof mascaras

Great for beach days or weddings, but they can be drying. Removing them is a chore too, so they shouldn't be worn every day.

Eyeliners

Used to line under and above the eyes, these should be soft and smudgy to ensure you don't need to scrub at the eyes when applying.

Left:
Eyeliner pencils.

Liquid eyeliners

These may need a steady hand to apply, but nothing says sexy eyes better.

Brow gel

Most of us ignore our eyebrows but they really define the face. Brow gel helps keep them in shape.

Eye make-up remover

It's essential to remove eye make-up with a specialist remover. Try to find one that's oil-free.

Eyeshadow brush

A flat, centimetre-wide eyeshadow brush is great for applying soft-looking shadow. A short handle gives more control and helps stop flecks falling on your cheeks.

Eyeshadow applicator

For more intense looks, sponge applicators give a greater depth of colour. Choose one with a soft foam tip and a short handle.

From top:
Powder eyeshadows; mascara brushes; liquid eyeliner brush; liquid eyeliner pen.

Eyelash comb

If you want to apply mascara without clumping, an eyelash comb is a must. Use it while lashes are still wet. You can buy metal eyelash combs, but plastic is safer because it isn't as sharp. And always brush downwards to lessen the risk of scratching your eyes.

Eyelash curlers

Curling eyelashes will help make your eyes look wider and brighter. Metal curlers are better than plastic; you should replace your curlers (or at least the pad that touches the eyelid) every six months.

False eyelashes

These are a great way to get instant glamour. Full sets are much easier to apply than individual lashes.

TOP 5 COLOUR TRICKS FOR EYES

• Blue liner placed along the lower lid of the eye will make red eyes look whiter.

• Dark shadows make eyes recede. Use them on prominent eyes or in areas you want to shade, like the socket crease. Light colours or shimmer make eyes look bigger and bring the area you use them on forward. They're great for deep-set eyes or to highlight brow bones.

• Avoid wearing shadows the same shade as your eye colour; they'll make your eyes disappear.

• A dot of shimmery shadow in the middle of the lid makes the eyes stand out on the face; a dot on the inside corner will make close-set eyes look further apart.

Left: Fake eyelashes.
Right: Eyelash curlers.

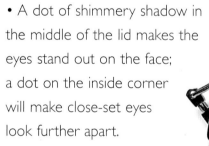

• If your eyeshadow always creases (which can happen on oily skins), try a sparkle. As the surface never looks flat, lines won't show as much.

TOP 5 APPLICATION TRICKS FOR EYES

• How you apply mascara depends on the colour of your lashes. If you have blonde lashes you need to make sure you get the colour right into the roots. This means using the wand vertically at first to colour right by the base of the lashes. Now you just brush through with the wand. If you have darker lashes then apply normally, sweeping from root to tip.

• If you want to wear two coats of mascara, make sure you apply the second before the first has dried – otherwise you'll create clumping. Then comb the lashes.

• If you're using dark shadow, apply eye make-up before putting on your foundation. This prevents specks falling onto your foundation. Or alternatively apply a layer of translucent face powder under the eye and sweep this off (along with any specks) when you've finished making up your eyes. But be warned – this only works if you use totally matt, colourless powder. Otherwise, you'll get white circles under the eyes – especially in photographs.

• Don't pump the mascara wand in and out of the tube in an attempt to get more colour on it. This will simply introduce air into the tube and dry out the mascara.

• Never apply liner inside the eyelid. Little clumps can break off and tear the film of the eye, causing irritation.

how to apply basic eye make-up

No matter what eye shades you're using, this technique will create a flattering make-up look with colour that really lasts.

1 Prime your eyelid. Eyeshadow will last longer if it's not applied directly to bare skin (oil on the lids can cause shadow to crease, while dry lids will absorb moisture from the shadow, leaving blotchy colour), so sweep foundation or concealer over the top.

2 Fill in your brows. Choose an eyebrow pencil that's the same colour or, if you're blonde or a redhead and have very pale brows, one shade darker than your natural brow colour. Using light strokes, gently colour over your brows to add emphasis.

3 Choose your shades. For this look you need a light shadow, a medium and a dark. It doesn't matter what they are so long as they go together. Try ivory, dove grey and charcoal on cool skins; taupe, beige and chocolate brown on warm. Dust the lightest shade across the whole of your eye, lid and socket.

4 Now, take the medium shade and apply this to the eye socket and the outer corner. Blend well using your finger.

5 Take the darkest shade and, using your sponge applicator, apply a thin line of this along the top lid and around the bottom as close to the lashes as you can get. Blend this well with another applicator or a cotton bud to create a smudgy line. Apply lashings of mascara.

EASY EYE TIPS

You can use make-up to bring out your eyes. If you have small or close-set eyes, follow the steps above but, when you get to Step 5, don't take the shadow all the way along the lower lid. This will shrink the eyes. Instead, concentrate the colour around the outer corner of the eye, blending to a soft tapered finish around the middle of the lower lid. Now add a tiny dab of shimmery or light shadow in the middle of the upper lid and blend well. Curl eyelashes or use a curling mascara to maximize the amount of eye you can see. If you want to bring out deep-set eyes, apply a light shade across the whole eyelid but skip the darker shade in the socket crease. Now take a dark but soft shade (like plum, deep brown or grey) and smudge this along the lower lid and outer corner of the eye. Line as before. Curl the eyelashes and apply lots of thickening mascara.

how to define eyes

There are a number of techniques you can use that will define your eyes more clearly. Try these tricks and make sure they really stand out.

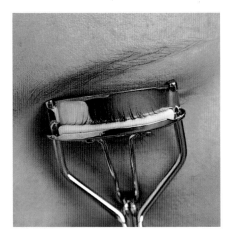

Applying liquid eyeliner

1 Hold the eyeliner brush between your thumb and forefinger, resting your hand on your cheek. Apply the liner in one swoosh as close to the lash line as you can, moving quickly from the inner corner out.

2 Stop the line at the end of your eyelid or go slightly up at the sides to create a catlike look. Be careful the line doesn't extend downwards, as this will make your eyes look sad.

3 If things go wobbly, don't hit the make-up remover. Instead get blending with a cotton bud and create a sultry smudged effect.

Curling your eyelashes

1 Make sure eyelashes are free of all mascara – curling hard lashes can make them snap.

2 Take your eyelash curlers and place them as close to the base of your lashes as possible.

3 Squeeze gently – too hard and you'll bend your lashes, not curl them. Hold for five seconds, then release.

4 Apply mascara.

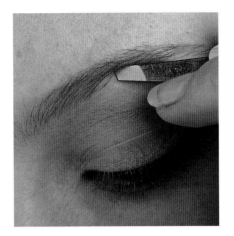

Applying false eyelashes

1 Before you do anything else you need to trim the lash strip to fit your eye – fake lashes should only go where real ones grow and that's not way down into your crow's feet. Measure them against your eye, holding it where your natural lashes end. Removing it from your face (or you might blind yourself), cut the excess off with nail scissors.

2 Usually a tube of glue is included in the pack when you buy your false eyelashes. Run a small line of it (preferably colourless) over the edge of the lashes.

3 Look down in the mirror: using tweezers, start from the outside corner and place the lashes as close to the base of your own lashes as possible.

4 Gently press with a cotton bud to seal the lashes into place.

5 Apply eyeshadow or even liquid eyeliner over the join.

How to pluck eyebrows

1 Find where your brow should go. To do this take a long eyeshadow brush and hold it straight up, resting lightly against your nostril. Where the tip meets the brow is where it should start.

2 Now find the end of your brow by holding the brush diagonally into the brow from the corner of your eye. Where the inside edge of the pencil hits is where your brow should end.

3 The best eyebrows have a slight arch. To work out where yours should go, hold the brush so the inside edge is on the outside of your iris (the coloured part of your eye). Where the brush meets the eyebrow is the point where the highest part of your brow should be.

4 Now it's time to pluck. Using the brightest light and best mirror you've got, pluck any stray hairs. Remember to pull quickly and in the direction of hair growth. Wipe over the brows with a little witch hazel. This will sterilize the open follicles.

EYES Q & A

Let us help you with your most common eyecare questions.

Q: I wake up every morning with puffy eyes. I always remove my make-up, so what am I doing wrong?
A: The most common reason for this happening is that you're removing your make-up with greasy removers. These leave an oily film on the eye and overnight this creates irritation that leads to puffiness. To avoid this, switch to oil-free make-up removers.

Q: I find I come home from work with red, bloodshot eyes. I've been using eye drops every day but my friend says these are bad for me. Why?
A: Eye drops beat red eyes by constricting the blood vessels within the eye. The only problem is that if they do this too often it weakens the blood vessels, making them more prone to redness. A better solution is to fight the cause of your redness. This is most likely to be dryness from staring at your computer all day. When we use a computer we tend to open our eyes wide and blink less often than normal, and this increases dehydration. Try to take breaks every 15 minutes – even if it's just to stare at something in the distance, and to blink 10 or 20 times.

Q: I always smudge my mascara when I put it on. What can I do?

A: One top make-up artist is known to bend all his mascara brushes at a right angle before he uses them, claiming this gives better aim and prevents smudging. Also, make sure you don't blink until mascara is dry – wait at least five seconds before letting go.

Q: I've got to start wearing glasses and am wondering if I should change my eye make-up?

A: The answer to this depends on how your sight is affected. If you are short-sighted, your eyes are going to be magnified under your glasses, so it's important that your application techniques are perfect (clumpy mascara will really show). If you're far-sighted your glasses can make your eyes look smaller, so you may need to lighten up eyeshadow shades a tone or two to make your eyes look larger. But whichever you have, don't go out without mascara or without defining your eyebrows. Both will help make your eyes stand out despite your glasses, and you won't disappear.

Q: My eyeshadow never lasts long enough. How can I make it stay where I want it to?

A: If you've followed our step-by-step advice on page 152 you'll know that priming your lids will help lengthen the life of your eyeshadow. Another tip is to apply a cream shadow (in the same shade) under your powder shadow. This creates a deeper shade of colour and will help both of them to stay put.

lips

No make-up look is complete without lip colour. Lipstick, lip gloss or even just a slick of lip liner will balance heavy eye looks and give focus to the face when you're using more neutral eye shades. However, while most of us take time on our eyes and use the right tools for our base, lips are often just dashed on with the stub of a lipstick. Also, despite the fact that they are one of the parts of the body with the thinnest skin and the least natural moisture, we rarely include lips as part of a skincare regime. The result is that many of us end up with chapped or dry lips, spend hours reapplying colour as our lip shades never stay put, and never really make the most of one of the focal points of our face. Well, that doesn't have to be the case. Creating a perfect pout is actually pretty easy.

the lipcare equipment kit

Creating perfect lips takes the right equipment – here's what you'll need.

Lip balm

Moisturizing product that helps prevent dryness. The best contain sunscreen, the worst contain camphor or menthol, which dry out the lips.

Flannel

Perfect for removing dry or flaky skin from the lips gently.

Lip liner

Used to create a perfect lip outline and help lipstick last longer. For the best results, warm in the palm of your hand before you use it.

Lip brush

The only way to apply lipstick like a pro. The perfect lip brush is thin and flat with a slightly pointed tip and long handle.

Lip gloss

Clear or coloured, this offers sheer, shiny coverage. Use it alone or on top of matt shades to give them shine.

Frosted lipstick

Shimmery and iridescent, this is perfect for evening looks. It should really be avoided on mature skins as it can highlight wrinkles and liplines.

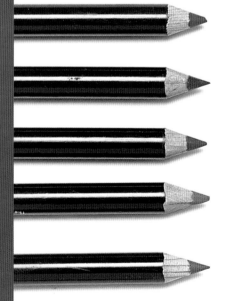

Left:
Lip liner pencils

Matt lipstick

Creates an intense, solid colour, but as it has little shine it will also contain few moisturizing ingredients. Always apply lip balm before you use it.

Satin lipstick

More coloured and less sticky than gloss, it still offers a shiny finish. It is more moisturizing than matt lipstick, but will need more frequent application.

Lip pencils

Softer and chubbier than lip liners, these are perfect for creating quick definition. They do have a tendency to dry the lips, however, so it's best to stick to neutral or shimmery shades – dark shades show up flaking more.

Lip stain

Normally liquid, it offers sheer but exceptionally long-lasting coverage. Don't use liner with it, just apply straight to the lips.

Lip sealant

Good for setting very bright, matt colours, but be careful – it contains lots of chemicals, which makes it unsuitable for sensitive skins. It can also be drying.

Clockwise from top: Lipsticks; lip gloss pots.

TOP 5 TIPS FOR LIPS

• If you decide a lipstick is too bright for you once you've got it on – but scrubbing it off will ruin your foundation – mix a little foundation with Vaseline and smear this over the shade with your fingertip to mute it.

• For emergency rehydration, pierce a vitamin E capsule, squeeze out the contents and apply to lips.

• If your lip gloss is too gooey, run an ice cube over your lips. It'll keep the shine, but stop that sticky sensation.

• Dark, matt lipsticks sometimes stain the lips. If this happens, rub the lips with olive oil.

• Lip (and tooth) brushes should be washed after contact with cold sores – or even when you have a cold – as they can reinfect you.

TOP 5 COLOUR TRICKS FOR LIPS

• Orangey red lipsticks will highlight yellowy teeth, while bluey reds make them look whiter.

• Light shades – particularly shimmery or frosted ones – will make lips look bigger.

• Dark shades or very matt colours will make lips look smaller.

• If you are fairly tanned you should choose a slightly darker shade of lipstick than you would without your tan or you can look washed out.

• Using sheer lipsticks and lip stains is an ideal way for the nervous to branch out into deep shades like plums, raisins and reds.

how to apply lipstick

If you don't want to be forever reapplying your lipstick, it is essential to learn the right way to put it on. These techniques will create lips that stay put.

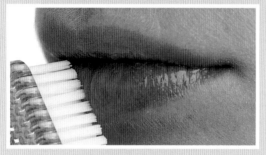

Basic lipstick application

1 Apply vaseline, then use a soft toothbrush to remove dead skin cells, brushing gently.

2 Apply your foundation as you normally would, making sure you lightly cover your lips too.

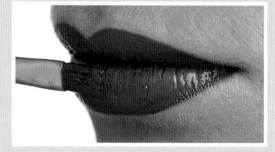

3 Apply lip liner that matches either your lips or your lipstick exactly. To apply it straight, rest your little finger on your chin and press the flattest side of the liner point on the middle of your Cupid's bow. Draw to the corner, sticking just inside the natural line of your lips. Once completed, colour the rest of the lips with the pencil.

4 Apply your lipstick with a lipbrush, blending again from the middle down to the corners of the mouth. If you're using a very bright colour make sure you go right into the corners.

5 Blot with tissue. Now reapply another coat of your lip colour. Blot again. Add lip sealant or lip gloss if required.

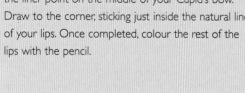

Make lips look bigger

Draw your liner along the outside of your lip line – but never lose contact with that line or things will look exceptionally artificial. Use a shimmery lip colour which makes lips look bigger or dab a little gold eyeshadow in the centre of your lips and blend outwards.

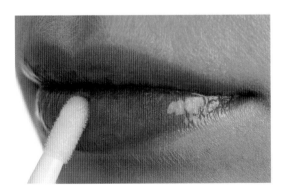

For sheer natural lips

Skip the liner and apply your lipstick direct to the lips with a brush – or for a longer-lasting look, choose a liner the same shade as your lips and apply this all over. Top with a little sheer lip gloss.

To even up lips

Don't try and create a totally fake lip line – it will probably go wonky. Instead use foundation over the lips as before, then draw along the outer edge of the lip line on the smaller lip and either just under or along the lip line of the bigger (depending on which will even up the difference more). Fill in the whole lip with liner so you're not left with tell-tale lines if your lipstick wears away.

LIPS Q & A

Let us help you with your most common lipcare questions.

Q: My lips are always cracked and dry. What should I do?

A:. You can either remove dry skin from your lips using a toothbrush (described on page 164), or you can use the edge of a damp flannel. Afterwards apply plenty of lip balm. Before you start to slick, however, check your brand doesn't contain camphor or methol, as this will make your problem worse with every application. Choose brands without either ingredient and with an SPF of at least 15 – lips are highly prone to sunburn.

Q: My lips are great but I get cold sores. What can I do?

A: Cold sores can be stopped in their tracks with over-the-counter treatments containing an active ingredient called aciclovir. The trick to it is to apply the treatment as soon as you feel that first tell-tale tingle. To help reduce attacks, wear an SPF lip balm. The cold sore virus is often triggered by sun exposure.

Q: I get cracks at the corners of my lips. Why does this happen?

A: The most common cause of this is vitamin B deficiency. Eat more wholegrain foods, eggs, red meat and also leafy green vegetables.

Q: I always get lipstick on my teeth. How do I prevent this?

A: The model's tip is to apply your lipstick as normal, then pop your finger in your mouth. Close your lips round it and pull your finger out. It'll take excess lipstick from the edge of your lips with it.

Q: How do I stop my lipstick from 'bleeding'?

A: This occurs when tiny lines start to form around the edge of the lips – it's very common in smokers. You can prevent it by always lining your lips when you wear lipstick. Glossy lipsticks are more prone to bleeding than matt or long-lasting colours, so switch to these. What's more, reds will bleed more than browns or pinks, as the way they are manufactured makes them naturally more prone to melting.

Q: Why does my lipstick look great when I try it in the shop and dreadful when I get it home?

A: Don't try it on the back of your hand, which is normally a different colour from your face and also a different texture. Obviously hygiene means testing lipsticks on your lips is a no-go, but your fingertips are closer in colour and texture, so try testing here instead.

make-up looks

On the next few pages you'll find a range of make-up looks designed to suit different occasions and environments, from the office to a dressy evening function.

Natural look

This does not mean going out without make-up – it just means using careful colour choices to enhance what nature has given you.

• Apply moisturizer and conceal any obvious blemishes. If you have good skin, forgo foundation and just sweep over loose powder. If you prefer to wear foundation, apply it with a slightly damp sponge, as this will soften the look and create a dewy sheen. Apply blusher just to the apples of your cheeks.

• Using an eyeshadow brush, sweep a soft pink or tawny-brown (almost blush-coloured) shadow across your lid and in the socket crease. This shouldn't be solid colour, just a slight brightening of the eye area. The key to the look is to shade only a line around the upper lashes and underneath the outer corner of the eye with a medium-shade eyeshadow. Eyes are a very important part of the natural look; too bare and you'll appear unmade up, too heavy and it'll seem like the rest of your make-up is half finished. Smudge this so it's very soft and apply brown or brown-black mascara.

• Apply a matt lipstick or a chubby lip pencil in a shade one darker than your natural lip colour.

Five-minute work look

You're late – or just fancy a lie-in. But your look needn't suffer with this speedy shape-up.

• Apply foundation or just dab concealer on any obvious blemishes and to cover any under-eye shadows.

• Sweep a neutral eyeshadow in taupe, beige or dove grey across your eyelid.

• Apply two coats of mascara.

• Apply blusher to the apple of your cheeks to create an instant glow.

• Shade your lips with a chunky lip pencil in a nude or rose-pink shade. This gives you precise lines and long-lasting colour in seconds.

Five-minute work to evening

You can even adapt your super-quick make-up look to take you from desk to dance floor.

• Cleanse your skin and reapply your foundation. Putting new base over old takes longer than starting again.

• Sweep your neutral shadow back over the lid. Now use a sponge applicator to smudge a darker shadow along the top of your upper lid and under your lower lashes. Aim for a soft line. Apply mascara.

• Reapply your blusher to the apples of your cheek. Sculpt up towards your cheekbones to create a more elegant, evening-friendly look.

• Put your neutral pencil on, then add a slick of lip gloss. The sheen adds glamour but doesn't take the time that a perfect evening lip in a dark shade needs.

Sexy party look

Heavy smoky eyes look difficult to achieve, but once you know how, you'll find that creating a striking party look is no problem at all.

• Apply foundation and loose powder for a flawless matt face.

• Grab a shimmery dark grey, black or bitter-chocolate brown shadow and sweep it across your eyelid. This will make sure that the focus of your look is your eyes.

• Use a soft kohl eyeliner in black and line the whole of your eyes. Don't worry about being too precise but get as close to the lashes as possible. Use a cotton bud to smudge all the way round – you want soft, blurred eyes, not harsh lines.

• Finish off the eyes with two coats of curling mascara.

• Apply blusher to the apples of your cheeks and then sweep this up into your hairline to give a sexy slant to your cheekbones.

• Apply lipstick. Brave girls should go for bright reds; those who want their eyes to do the talking should stick with soft pinks or nude shades.

Sophisticated style

This look is for day or evening and is most definitely designed to impress.

• Using concealer and a liquid or cream-to-powder foundation, apply a full base.

• Apply blusher – pronounced cheekbones are key to the look. Sweep your blusher up along your cheekbones or, to make them stand out further, just underneath, adding a little highlighter on the cheekbone itself.

• Using a dark neutral colour like grey, brown or black, shade your upper eyelid and the eye crease. Now apply a light shade across the brow bone.

• Sweep liquid eyeliner across your upper eyelid – at night, extend this about two millimetres past the eyelid line in a little flick. This creates a cat's-eyes look.

• Apply mascara.

• During the day use natural shades for lips that are just one or two tones darker than your unmade-up lips. In the evening go for brighter, more striking tones. Lips need to be perfectly lined and matt, so it really is worth taking your time on them. Remember always to use a lip brush.

Sun-kissed look

Creating that 'just back from holiday' look is simple – even when the sun's gone down.

• Break the foundation first rule and start by applying concealer to any obvious blemishes.

• Apply a little tinted moisturizer all over your face to give a light sheen.

• Take a tawny-brown or browny-pink blusher and apply this very lightly to the apples of your cheeks, the tip of your nose, the tip of your chin and around your hairline.

• Apply a shadow with a little shimmer in it to your eyelids. Good colours for this include golds, bronzes, browns and beiges. Apply brown or black mascara.

• If you're a blonde or redhead, define your brows. Colour on the face can make them disappear, so brush them lightly with some eyeshadow in the same shade or one tone darker than their natural colour.

• Apply a shade of lipstick just one tone darker than your natural lip colour. Now, brush over this lightly with a little frosted lipstick, shimmery pale shadow or lip gloss to create a light, sheeny look.

5

your body

Beauty is a whole-body experience

– from the de-stressing value of a long hot bath to the practicality of hair removal, looking good does not stop at your chin. The problem, however, is that a huge number of us don't like the bits under our chin. We're too fat, too thin, not busty enough or a bit saggy, and because of this dissatisfaction most of us try not to pay much attention to these parts of our bodies. It's a head in the sand approach, and according to US-based positivity expert Ann Kearney-Cooke, it is actually self-defeating. The more time we spend looking at our bodies, the more we will begin to like them. And what better way to get to know your body than by spoiling and pampering it with beauty regimes? By spending a little time on bodycare every day you will not only create a sense of total well-being but also, in some cases, improve your overall health. And let's face it, a healthy body is the most beautiful body of all.

the bodycare equipment kit

Looking after your body properly takes the right equipment – here's what you'll need.

Bath foams

The most common form of bath additive, they are best for those with oily skins as they can dehydrate.

Bath oils

Best for dry skins, these leave a layer of oil on the skin's surface which helps a lot with rehydration.

Mineral or sea salts

Renowned for their relaxing and rehydrating properties, mineral salts from areas like the Dead Sea help balance the body.

Seaweed baths and masks

Again, detoxifying and moisturizing, seaweed-based bath products are used in the world's top health spas.

Aromatherapy oils

Either blended or used alone, a few drops of essential oil in a bath make it a relaxing and therapeutic experience.

Mud masks

Usually from the Dead Sea, mud baths and masks contain high levels of minerals which detox and moisturize the body. Many Dead Sea products have been found to help with psoriasis and eczema.

Body lotion

A must after a bath or shower to help replace any water lost and seal in any left on the skin. Apply it while skin is still slightly damp.

Anti-cellulite gels/creams

Contain ingredients that tone, firm and act on fat to help reduce the appearance of cellulite.

Fake tans

The only safe way to get that golden glow. There are many different types and choosing the best one for you is very important.

Hair removers

Like fake tans, choosing from the many varieties of these is important if you don't want your skin smoothing to become a chore.

Loofah

Used to remove dead skin cells and help boost circulation, loofahs can be harsh on sensitive skin but are great on very dry patches or for overall exfoliation on other skin types. Just make sure you dry them between uses – they can carry bacteria otherwise.

Body scrub

Normally has larger or rougher granules than facial scrub – body skin can take more scrubbing than the delicate skin of the face.

Body brush

Used to help speed circulation and so remove toxins from the body, they're an important part of cellulite control.

Clockwise from right: Loofah; pumice; body brush.

183

water-baby beauty

The healing power of water has been used in beauty therapy for years. Here's how to use your bath or shower to relax, soothe, smooth, energize or detox your body.

Relaxing

The ultimate relaxing bath is around 38 degrees Centigrade; this is the temperature that's been shown to relax the muscles and stimulate the production of calming chemicals in the brain. Add soothing bath oils containing scents like lavender, melissa or patchouli.

• Before you get in the bath gently exfoliate with a loofah, as this will help your body absorb relaxing oils a lot more effectively.
• Turn down the lights, pop some candles round the bath if you like, or float some flower petals on the top.
• Stay in there for 20 to 30 minutes, enjoying the peace and silence.

Soothing

Back and shoulder aches seem to be a common part of many people's working lives but you can help to heal these things in the bath.

Epsom or sea salts contain ingredients that, when absorbed by the body, have an anti-inflammatory action. Add to this the healing benefits of hot water and it's easy to see how a bath can soothe away the aches and pains of the day.

• Run water of around 38 degrees Centigrade and add some Epsom salts or mineral-based bath salts.
• Lie under the water and try a spot of hydrotherapy. Turn the shower head on at full blast and put it into the water, directing the jet onto your back and shoulders to give an excellent underwater massage.

Smoothing

Baths can help you create super smooth skin, if you know how. Try out the following suggestions:

• Start with damp skin and apply an exfoliating scrub to remove the dead skin cells.

• Run a bath that's warm enough to sit in comfortably, but not too hot (hot water will only dehydrate the skin).
• Add a pint of milk or cream. These contain ingredients like whey protein which hydrate the skin.
• Relax for 20 minutes (the optimum time for hydration) and gently massage the water into your skin.
• Get out and lightly pat yourself dry.
• Before the last drops of water absorb into your skin, apply a rich body lotion.

Energizing

Most of us use the bath to relax and the shower to give us that get up and go, but it doesn't have to be that way. Sitz baths (where the upper and lower body are exposed to different temperatures) have been used for years to energize and invigorate the body. Here's how to create the effect.

• Run a bath warm enough to sit in. Put in energizing bath foams or oils concentrating on scents like lemon, orange or grapefruit.

• Before you get in, brush your body vigorously to start your circulation soaring. Use firm quick strokes, moving up towards the heart.

• Get in the bath and relax for five to ten minutes with a cup of peppermint or green tea, with your feet at the end near the taps.

• Start running cold water over your feet to boost your metabolism and to energize. Get out when the water has cooled.

• Apply body lotion and you'll be set to face the day.

Detox

Normally, we take baths to make us clean. Here's how to do some serious, deep-down cleansing.

• Make sure your bathroom is warm enough and start off with an empty bath. Using a few handfuls of damp sea salt, exfoliate your body from head to toe using big circular movements.

• Rinse this off, then towel-dry well.

• Apply a mud or seaweed mask to your whole body for a great detox (don't worry if things start to get messy!) and wrap yourself in a towel – preferably one you don't mind getting filthy. Even better, get someone to wrap your body in a bin bag (obviously keeping your head well clear).

• Relax for 20 minutes.

• Shower off the mask and then run a warm bath.

• Add more seaweed mixture or some green clay (which you'll find at many health food stores).

• Relax for 15 to 20 minutes.

• Finish with a blast of cold water to boost your circulation.

TOP 5 TIPS
FOR BATHING

• Enhance the action of your bath with essential oils. Six drops in the water are enough to make a difference. Try grapefruit, bergamot or lime to energize; clary sage, rosemary or patchouli to soothe your mind; and melissa, lavender or camomile to send you to sleep.*

• If you're using essential oils, put them in once you have finished running the water. Close the door and wait two to three minutes before you get in – this helps the oils evaporate into the air and maximizes their powers.

• For the best beauty results, baths should be either long or short. Short baths (five to ten minutes) cleanse the skin without dehydration, while if you stay in the bath for over 20 minutes you'll start to rehydrate your skin from outside (the reason you go pruny).

• On the other hand, baths that last between 10 and 20 minutes should be avoided, as you actually lose water from the skin while you bathe. This can result in dehydration.

• Just a couple of words of warning: if you are allergic to seafood, skip seaweed baths. If you have sensitive skin, body brushing, salts, essential oils or bath foams are best avoided. If you have any heart or blood pressure problems avoid very hot or very cold baths or showers.

* If you are pregnant or epileptic check with your doctor before using any oils.

MAKE YOUR BATH BOUNTIES

It's easy to whip up soothing bath treatments from the ingredients of your own kitchen.

Moisturizing body treatment

For a moisturizing pre-bath body treat mix together the following ingredients:

½ cup finely ground almonds
1 cup porridge oats/oatmeal
1 avocado (mashed)

Rub the mixture into the body, leave for five minutes, shower off, then have a moisturizing bath.

Super-scrub

Create a super-powered body scrub with fruits containing fruit acids. These help dissolve dead skin cells, which can then be whisked away. Mix the following:

1 guava
1 kiwi
handful Dead Sea salts
2 tbsp honey

Apply to the body in circular motions.

Rich bath remedy

For a rich moisturizing bath blend use the following ingredients:

1 cup oatmeal
3 cups powdered milk

Add the oatmeal to the milk in a muslin bag. Place this under the tap and run the water through it.

hair removal

The average woman has around 11,000 hairs on her legs and 2,500 under her arms – here's how to find the best method for you to get rid of them!

Bleaching

What you need: bleach cream.

What it does: uses lightening ingredients to disguise hair.

Where: face and lower arms.

Lasts: up to two months.

Pain factor: nil – unless you leave it on too long.

Insider tip: never bleach immediately after using skin products containing alpha-hydroxy acids, because this can cause scarring.

How: wash the area to ensure there are no cosmetics on your skin that could react with the chemicals in the bleach. Apply as directed and for as long as stated. Wash off.

Tweezing

What you need: tweezers.

What they do: pull the hair out at the root.

Where: best for eyebrows.

Lasts: four to six weeks.

Pain factor: it hurts a little, but applying ice before you pluck will numb the pain.

Insider tip: for the best results choose tweezers with flat, slanted tips rather than pointy ones – they grasp the hair more easily and are less likely to scratch the skin.

How: quickly and in the direction of hair growth. To avoid overplucking brows, draw on the end shape you'd like to achieve and stick to this (see page 155 for more detail on this).

Shaving

What you need: razor.

What it does: cuts the hair at the surface of the skin.

Where: underarms and legs – bikini lines and facial hair aren't really appropriate for shaving as the hair grows back blunt, making it noticeable on the face and itchy on the bikini line.

Lasts: one to two days.

Pain factor: nil unless you slip, but using a single-blade razor minimizes the risk of cuts.

Insider tip: use hair conditioner instead of soap – it doesn't dehydrate your skin.

How: soak in the bath for two to three minutes before you shave. This expands the hair follicles, giving a closer, longer-lasting shave. Apply shaving foam or hair conditioner. Now shave upwards, then downwards. Rinse and moisturize.

Depilatory cream

What you need: a cream formulated for the area you're going to treat.

What it does: uses chemicals to dissolve the hair just under the skin's surface.

Where: anywhere.

Lasts: two to three weeks.

Pain factor: nil – though they can smell pretty horrid.

Insider tip: apply a little soya milk after you've removed the cream – ingredients called serine protease inhibitors stop hair growth and keep you smooth longer.

How: so simple. Apply as directed, wait as long as the directions tell you and shower off. Avoid hot water and perfumed products on the area for at least three hours after application to reduce the risk of irritation.

Waxing/Sugaring

What you need: prepared wax strips; hot wax used with cloth or sugaring solution (normally made from sugar or honey and lemon).

What it does: pulls the hair out right at the root.

Where: anywhere.

Lasts: four to six weeks.

Pain factor: pretty high, especially around your bikini line. Taking a mild painkiller like aspirin helps.

Insider tip: start waxing in winter – hair needs to be at least three millimetres long in order to be waxed properly and you're less likely to notice this in the winter months. Also, as each waxing thins hair, the regrowth will be less noticeable when the summer months arrive.

How: apply talc to dry up skin oils, which may prevent the wax sticking. Apply wax strips or hot wax and cloth. Leave for two or three seconds, then pull quickly in the direction of hair growth. Remove excess wax with warm water and avoid perfumed products for 48 hours.

cellulite

Doctors may debate whether or not cellulite exists, but if you suffer from that orange-peel effect on your bottom and thighs, you'll know it does.

The old theory was that cellulite was caused by toxins building up under the skin, but that's probably not true. It's more likely to be the result of poor skin structure, causing the fibres to split. This means fat and, yes, possibly toxins squish out through the holes in the fibres, creating that lumpy effect. In other words, your bottom is rather like an old mattress with the stuffing sticking out! Chances are the problem is genetic, and lies with the X chromosome (only women have this, which would explain why men don't get cellulite). While all this may mean cellulite isn't your fault, reducing its appearance *is* within your control. Strengthening the skin fibres, plumping the skin's surface and breaking down the stubborn fat and 'toxin' deposits can help minimize the look of cellulite. Here's our list of top techniques.

Body brushing

Some experts claim this is the key to total cellulite removal, saying it helps speed up the lymph system to remove toxins from the body. Of course, it depends on the whole cellulite/toxin theory being true; but as an active lymphatic system helps improve your skin anyway, there's no harm in trying it. For the best results, dampen your skin, then use a firm-bristled brush to stroke each limb briskly in the direction of the heart. Do this twice daily, but be careful – applying perfumed products directly afterwards can irritate. Wait at least half an hour before using any products.

Diet

Many different eating plans claim to beat cellulite, but there's no miracle cure – eating watermelon for three days won't make your thighs dimple-free.

Instead, the best anti-cellulite diet is rich in fruit and vegetables, which help flood the body with water but also contain essential skin-firming nutrients. It's low in fat (about 25 per cent of your daily calories should come from fat – that's around 50 grams a day). Finally, it's low in

'toxins' like caffeine, nicotine and alcohol. This will help if the theory on toxins is true, but more importantly these all dehydrate the skin, and dry skin shows cellulite more. You should also drink at least two litres of water a day.

Exercise

Not only does this burn the excess fat that can cause cellulite, it also increases blood flow to the surface of the skin and this plumps the skin, making it less noticeable. For the best results you need to do 30 to 60 minutes of aerobic exercise five or six times a week. Weights also help as they firm the muscles under the skin, which helps disguise cellulite. You should notice an improvement in six to 12 weeks.

Creams

The most important ingredients in cellulite creams now are those called phosphodiesterase inhibitors. In plain, simple English, these stop production of the enzyme that leads to fat storage in our body and so cause the dimples to shrink. Many ingredients have this effect, including caffeine, aminophylline, theophylline, kola nut and guarana. Alongside these are ingredients like menthol or butcher's broom, which help dilate blood vessels, increasing circulation in the area; gingko biloba which is said to firm the skin; and lemon and fennel, which help detox the body and repair skin. Apply the cream two hours after eating or one hour before – your body will only burn fat when it has none in the bloodstream.

Whatever happens, don't expect any improvements for six to eight weeks and don't expect the cellulite to disappear completely – the creams only ever promise to reduce it.

Moisturizer

Plumped-out skin shows cellulite less than dehydrated skin, so it's a good idea to incorporate body lotion application into your daily regime.

Sunscreen

Cellulite gets worse as collagen and elastin levels decrease in the body. If you always use sun protection you will slow that decrease, and add moisture too.

Fake tan

The darker your skin the less noticeable cellulite will be, as the shadows caused by the dimpling will be less obvious.

Massage

As with body brushing, massage is supposed to speed up the circulation, but kneading the cellulite areas is also supposed to help break down toxins and fat. Certainly, the only approved treatment for cellulite (endomologie) uses rollers to squish and squash the skin, though the pressure used is more intense than you'll ever manage on your own. If you have the time try it. Using your moisturizer, a cellulite cream or detoxifying massage oil, spend five to ten minutes on each area, rubbing, rolling and pressing the cellulite.

fake tan

In a recent survey, 51 per cent of people said they felt better about their body when it was tanned. They felt thinner, they felt sexier and they felt fitter.

Feeling confident about your body is one of the most beautiful states any woman can be in. However, as we know only too well, tanning comes at a price. Exposing yourself to the sun's ultraviolet rays ages the skin, adding up to 20 years to how you'll look by the time you reach your forties. On a more serious note, sunbathing can kill you by promoting a very serious form of skin cancer called malignant melanoma. Faking a tan is therefore one of the best things you can do for your body in terms of both beauty and health. Here's how.

Choosing your tanner

There are a number of different types of fake tan. If you're nervous, choose one you can wash off immediately.

• **Facial tans:** These are normally slightly lighter in consistency and shade than body tans. Also they are designed with fewer pore-blocking ingredients.

• **Bronzing gel:** Used to create a sheer facial tan, they wash off after use. Great if you're nervous about uneven application.

• **Temporary tanners:** These apply a bronze colour to the skin's surface but don't actually stain it. You can wash them off immediately, but they're no good to use while swimming.

• **Cream tans:** The most common form of fake tan, they contain an ingredient called DHA (dihydroxyacetone) which attaches to protein in skin, darkening it.

• **Spray tans:** These also contain DHA but are often in lighter formulations. They're also much easier to apply.

• **Tinted tans:** These are great when you want to avoid streaking. They go on dark, so you can see where you've applied the colour, then fade into the skin. A few hours later, the tan appears.

• **Tan enhancers:** These can be aftersun moisturizers, shower gels or cellulite creams but they all work in the same way, delivering a very low level of fake tan to the skin.

Choosing your shade

Fake tans come in different shades and choosing one that's too dark is a big mistake. You will find that tans come in two basic types.

- **Golden:** This is a yellow-based tan best for blondes, redheads, those with black hair, those with Asian-type or very pale skin, and anyone whose brown hair gets golden lights in summer.
- **Bronze:** This is for everyone else. Remember that your face never goes as dark as your body; keep it one to two shades lighter for a natural look.

Applying it well

It is very easy to apply fake tan badly, leaving you with a blotchy look. For the best results stick to these golden rules.

- **Exfoliate the skin:** Dry skin absorbs higher concentrations of fake tan, which means it ends up darker than the rest of you. The day (or at least two hours) before you decide to tan, go over your whole body with a body scrub. Pay special attention to elbows, knees and ankles. Now moisturize well to prevent any further dehydration. Don't do this just before you tan – if the moisturizer isn't applied properly or dried properly, it's a sure-fire way to getting a streaky, uneven tan.

- **Apply the tan:** Work on one limb at a time. For the best results wear gloves (to prevent orange palms) and rub the tan in circular motions (this reduces streaking) until it's totally absorbed into the skin. Don't skimp, as patchy application leads to a patchy look, but use less than if you were applying body lotion. You shouldn't be left with excess on the skin. Dry areas like elbows, ankles and knees should always be treated last and with minimum product – just use what's left on your palms.
- **Do hands last:** The best way is to rub tan on the back of one hand, then rub the two backs of your hands together. If you do decide to use your palms, rub them straight away with a wipe soaked in toner – nothing says fake tan like orange palms.
- **Eliminate streaks:** Use astringent toners to remove fake tan, or try using toothpaste. Exfoliation will even out patchy application.
- **Repeat the process:** If you feel you're not dark enough once the product has been completely absorbed into your skin, apply another coat of fake tan as described above.

eat your way to a better body

When it comes to the shape and condition of your body, you are most definitely what you eat. Diet can help beat fat and fluid retention and protect you against sun damage.

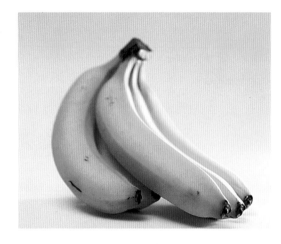

To lose weight

Losing weight is a matter of eating fewer calories than you burn. To do this means knowing how many calories you use in a day. To work it out, multiply your weight in kilograms by 0.9 and multiply that total by 24. This is how many calories you use to fuel your body every day. Of course, moving around also uses calories and you need to account for these. If you have a sedentary job and do no exercise, add 25 per cent to that figure; if you have a sedentary job but exercise hard for at least 30 minutes a day, add 40 per cent to that figure; if you are in a very active job or exercise heavily add 60 per cent.

This is how many calories you use a day, and eating 500 fewer than this a day will mean a safe weight loss of half a kilogram a week. For the best results you should follow a diet high in fruit and vegetables and low in fat, with moderate protein and carbohydrate intake. Try following the plate portion rule: for every meal ensure half of your plate is fruit or vegetables (not including potatoes), the other half part lean protein (white meat, fish, low-fat dairy products, tofu, beans or pulses) and part carbohydrate (bread, pasta, rice, potatoes, couscous).

To gain weight

Of course, not everyone needs to lose weight – some of us would actually like to gain weight. It's actually harder to do this healthily than you may think – the foods that contain the most calories are normally the ones that are particularly bad for our health.

To gain half a kilogram means eating 3,500 calories more than normal; to do this safely, eat high-nutrient, high-calorie snacks like nuts and seeds, increase servings of healthy carbohydrates like bread, pasta, rice and couscous (rather than sugary carbs), and incorporate smoothies made from milk or yoghurt with blended fruits like bananas or strawberries. All of these will increase your calorie intake but won't overload you with fat or empty nutrients.

To beat fluid retention

Fluid retention hits most women prior to their period. It leads to a bloated belly, swollen painful breasts, and for some women swollen fingers and face too. The cure for it is probably not what you think — you need to drink water and eat more water-filled foods. Fluid retention is caused when the body is triggered into thinking water is short so it holds fluid in the body; however, if you are constantly supplying it with water this doesn't happen. Also, avoid diuretic substances (like caffeine and alcohol) and be very careful about your salt intake. Salt dramatically increases fluid retention. Finally, many women find evening primrose oil helps fight fluid retention. Take a supplement every day.

To protect your skin

Never leaving the house without sunscreen should be your number-one beauty rule, but you can also build your own sunscreen by loading up your body with anti-oxidant nutrients like vitamins A, C and E. Recent American research showed that eating 10 portions of fruit and vegetables (particularly those coloured red, yellow or orange) every day for six weeks helped build an anti-oxidant layer under the skin that was equivalent to SPF4 sunscreen. While this doesn't mean you can go without your UV screen, it will help mop up any rays that do get through — plus, those nutrients have many other important functions in the body, so they won't go to waste.

BODY Q & A

Let us help you with your most common bodycare questions.

Q: Why do I get annoying ingrown hairs when I wax?
A: These little hairs that curl back under the skin are just one of those girly facts of life. However, you can prevent them by gently exfoliating with a loofah every day. This eases the hairs out and helps them grow in the right direction.

Q: I've got really scaly skin on my calves which doesn't disappear when I moisturize. What it is it?
A: It's actually cell renewal gone berserk. Your skin is renewing at a faster rate than normal, creating the dry, scaly look. Strange but true, the best way to treat it is scrubbing with a little sugar paste. Sugar contains an ingredient which slows down the desquamation (as it's known in beauty circles).

Q: The backs of my arms are covered in little red bumps. I don't get spots anywhere else, so I can't understand these at all.
A: These are actually a form of dry skin rather than spots. The most common cure is to increase levels of essential fatty acids (found in oily fish, nuts and seeds) in your diet.

Q: What should I do about spider veins on my legs?
A: These little red or purple veins normally occur after exposure to hot and cold temperatures, because of hormonal fluctuations or just as a side effect of ageing. The most common treatment is called sclerotherapy and it involves injecting a salt solution into the vein which makes it swell and seals it up. It's very effective. Laser treatments can also now help spider veins, but it is more painful and more pricy.

Q: Can you prevent stretch marks when you're pregnant?

A: Stretch marks occur when the skin grows at too rapid a rate for its fibres to handle. These tear, leaving purple, indented marks. They are often genetic. They are also more likely to occur the older you are when you are pregnant, as the skin is less elastic then. Keeping the skin moisturized with emollients like cocoa butter will help, but if they do hit, applying a glycolic acid-based alpha-hydroxy cream will lighten and smooth them. Don't do this while you're pregnant, though – you should use as few chemicals as possible then. Start once the baby is born.

Q: I've heard there's a supplement that can help prevent varicose veins. My mum has loads and I don't want them too.

A: Well, you're right that the tendency to varicose veins does seem to be inherited. They occur when the vein walls and valves weaken, and blood flows down the vein rather than up. This creates pooling and that blue, lumpy effect. Standing around for long periods tends to make them worse, while support stockings help prevent or improve them. However, new research says that horse chestnut can help strengthen the veins and lower the risk of varicose veins. Ask at a health food shop about gels or tablets.

6

hands & feet

If details make the difference then knowing how to look after your hands and feet is a vital part of the beauty experience. Neat, manicured nails and feet that look silky soft rather than dry and cracked are the finishing touch to all the rest of your grooming. Most of us, however, neglect these areas, thinking we don't have time to paint our nails – and that our feet are just too much like hard work. This

doesn't have to be the case. With simple regimes

designed to make the most of these areas, you really

can be beautiful from head to toe. After all, on

average your nails grow just over $\frac{1}{8}$ inch a month.

Start caring for them now and you can have inch-long

talons in no time.

hand- and footcare equipment kit

Looking after your hands and feet takes the right equipment – here's what you'll need.

Emery board

The best way to shape nails – the rough side is for shortening the nail, the smooth for final shaping and smoothing.

Orange and hoof sticks

Orange sticks are used with a little cotton wool on the end to push back cuticles. Hoof sticks are similar, but harder to use.

Cuticle cream or oil

Softens cuticles, helping keep them neat and less prone to hangnails. Used regularly, it will also help nails grow through more healthily.

Cuticle remover

Used to gently whittle away excess cuticle skin.

Nail clippers

The best way to cut toenails and fingernails. Cut straight across.

Cuticle clippers

Only to be used to treat hangnails, as cutting the main cuticles can lead to infection in the nail bed.

Nail oils

Help hydrate and strengthen nails – look for those with almond oil, or try oil of elemi for ultimate strengthening.

Nail polish remover

Should be acetone-free to prevent nails from drying.

Base coat

Protects from dehydration and also staining with bright or dark polishes.

Top coat

Used over nail polish to help prolong the life of a manicure or pedicure.

Nail polish

Not only does nail polish help add to your look, it also protects the nails from breaking or bending.

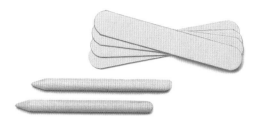

Stick-on false nails

Simple way to glam up your hands. They last one night.

Salon false nails

Made of hardened gel, these are painted on in the salon and last for weeks, until they are soaked off.

Pumice stone

For small areas of dry skin, a pumice stone used before bathing will help soften things up.

Foot file

Similar to a pumice, it offers a slightly harsher scrubbing action and is suitable for drier skin.

Sander

This little electrical tool is the only way to get rid of very dry or hard skin on the feet.

Hand cream

Use it every time you get your hands wet to help keep them hydrated and strengthen nails.

Foot cream

Needs to be thick and moisturizing to hydrate the very dry skin on the feet. Creams containing an ingredient called urea are best.

Toe separators

Help prevent polish smudging from nail to nail.

Left page: Toenail clippers; cuticle cream.
This page: orange sticks; emery boards;
french manicure set of nail varnishes;
toe separators; nail file.

what type of nails do you have?

Fed up with spending time on your nails only for them to snap minutes after your manicure? Well, if the products you're using aren't right for your nail type, you could actually be killing your nails with kindness. Truth is, just like skin and hair, nails come in types – five, in fact. Nails can be dry, brittle, damaged, soft or normal, and they need to be treated accordingly. Here's how to diagnose your particular nail type – and how to treat it properly.

Dry nails

Dry nails lack lustre and look dull; plus, if you run your thumb over the nail, it will drag slightly instead of sliding cleanly across. The secret to treating dry nails is to rehydrate them – vitamin E is fantastic for this (just like it is on dry skin) so open a vitamin capsule and rub it directly onto the nails morning and evening. It'll also help if you always wear a moisturizing base coat to hydrate the nails twenty-four/seven and prevent further drying by switching from soap to hand washes. Finally, steer clear of pearlized polish. The ingredients used to make them sparkly can be dehydrating.

Brittle nails

Gently press the sides of your nails together. If your nail doesn't bend, chances are you have brittle nails. These have no moisture left in them at all, which also means they have no flexibility and shatter as soon as they bash on something. This causes most people to reach for the nail hardener, but this is the worst thing you can do as it makes the nail even more rigid. It's better to boost flexibility by oiling the nails nightly with almond oil instead. The shape of your nails will also add strength. The best is a squoval shape (where the sides of the nail are left straight and only the top is rounded), as this helps the nail absorb shocks better.

Damaged nails

If your nails are flaking or splitting, you have damaged nails. These are most commonly caused by severe dehydration. Help them with a treatment base coat to heal the nail, but make sure that, as you apply it, you stipple it into any flaky spots (just like you would cover peeling paint). This will prevent air bubbles forming under the polish and stop flaking – which is important, as flaking polish takes nail cells with it, increasing damage.

You also need to ensure that the cells that grow through next time are strong and healthy, so use cuticle oil twice daily; if the cuticle is supple, the new cells can push through more easily, so they arrive at the nail bed in the best of health.

Soft nails

If your nails bend at the slightest touch and rarely grow past your fingertip you've got soft nails. To get them back into shape, you need to harden them up. The simple way to do this is to apply a nail hardener or try rubbing in a little essential oil of elemi (order this at health food stores). In fact, any oil will help strengthen soft nails as it keeps out their main enemy, water, which softens them even further.

Always wear gloves when you're washing up and apply hand cream after washing your hands.

Normal nails

If you have none of the above problems – your nails bend slightly when pressed, look pink and shiny and will grow easily – you're lucky, you naturally have normal nails. Try to keep them that way by moisturizing them regularly with hand creams, and avoiding harsh detergents and overly hot water.

TOP 5 TIPS
FOR NAILS

• Always wipe nails with a cloth before painting. Any oils left on the nail will prevent polish from sticking and increase the risk of chipping.

• If a nail chips, the best thing to do is remove the polish and start again. If you don't have time, dip your finger in nail polish remover and smooth it over the chipped area to soften the edges. Now, repaint that area and then cover with top coat to reseal the nail.

• If you smudge polish while it's drying, dab your fingertip in remover and use it to smooth the surface, then repaint with top coat.

• If nails break, the only thing you can do is cut them off. If, however, the break is low down, take a teabag and cut a tiny strip of the gauze. Apply this to the nail and paint over with polish.

• Don't apply nail polish remover to gunky nail varnish, as it will dry out the nail. Instead, use specialist thinners that are available from beauty stores.

TOP 5 COLOUR
TRICKS FOR NAILS

• Dark colours make nails look shorter. Beat this by leaving a white strip on the side of the nail as you paint.

• Small nails look bigger if you use shimmery or metallic polishes.

• Pale colours are best for girls in a hurry. They show fewer mistakes and chips are more easily disguised.

• To make unpainted or natural nails look longer, run a white nail pencil under the tip.

• Bluey red nail polishes can make mature hands look older. Stick to vibrant reds or paler shades.

MAKE YOUR HAND TREATMENT

Like the skin on your face, hand skin sometimes needs a little extra help. To brighten up dull hands you need to exfoliate. Make a rich exfoliating hand paste by mixing together the following ingredients:

2 tsp sugar
1 tbsp honey

Rub the honey paste over your hands and nails to remove dead skin cells. Rinse off, then moisturize.

MAKE YOUR NAIL FOOD

Warm a little olive oil in a pan over the stove. This should be only slightly hot; do not boil it and test it carefully before you use it. Now soak your hands and nails in the mixture for two to three minutes. Wipe off the excess, apply gloves and sit tight for an hour (it's even better if you do this overnight).

basic manicure

This is the absolute bread and butter of your nailcare regime. A regular manicure will give you strong, smooth and beautiful nails.

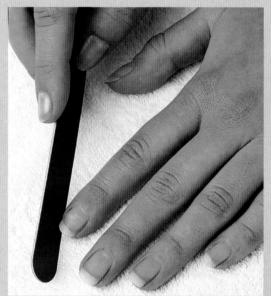

1 Remove old polish with a non-acetone polish remover.

2 File your nails into shape. The most protective and elongating shape is the squoval, where the sides are straight but the top is curved. To prevent damaging the nail layers you should file in only one direction, preferably from the outside into the middle.

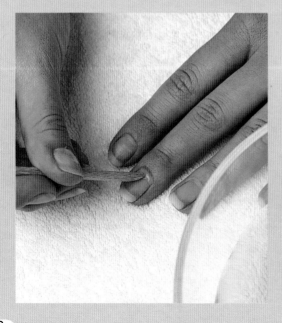

3 Soak your nails in a little warm water to soften the remaining cuticles and then gently push them back with an orange stick. The first time you do this you may have a lot of cuticle; in this case, apply a cuticle remover to each nail. Leave to work for two to three minutes, then wipe off. This will remove any excess without harming the nail bed. Wash your hands again and dry well.

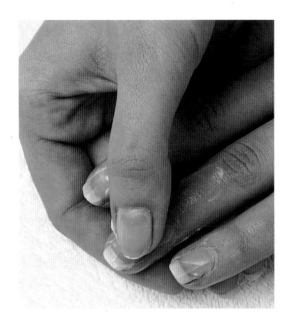

4 Apply hand cream to the hands and nails and wait two to three minutes. Now wipe each nail with a tissue to remove any excess.

5 Apply the base coat and leave to dry. Then apply polish. The best way to do this is with two or three thin coats. Start at the base of the nail and sweep up in one easy movement. Cover the middle of the nail first, then the edges. Any spills over the side can be wiped off with the orange stick dipped in a little nail polish remover.

6 Wait for the colour to dry, then cover the nail with a top coat. To help your colour last longer, apply this under the nail tip and along the nail tip as well. Leave for at least half an hour before touching – and remember, polish takes four to five hours to dry completely.

french manicure

This traditional manicure technique is used to enhance the contrast between the main part of the nail and the tip.

1 Shape nails and deal with cuticles as with the traditional manicure. Then apply base coat.

2 Now paint the whole nail with a neutral, pale shade which should match the natural colour of the nail bed. Leave this to dry.

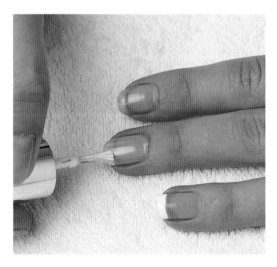

3 Paint the naturally white tip of the nail with an opaque white or beige polish. In traditional french manicures this white strip is straight across the tip of the nail; however, curving it to follow (or create) a natural oval will make the nails look longer.

4 Finish off the nail with a coat of clear varnish. This will protect the layers underneath, helping the manicure to last longer.

party nails

For a special night out, liven up your nails with these glamorous party looks and you're sure to stand out from the crowd.

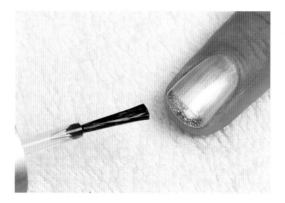

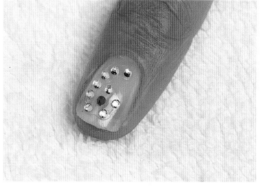

Mix and match

For this look use a french manicure technique with colours. You can use any colours you like, for instance: coat the nail in pale pink and apply fuchsia or purple to the tip, or try red nails tipped in black. For the ultimate in drama, tip shiny purple nails with glittery silver polish.

Nail jewels

Create a subtle party shimmer using delicate gems. Polish your little fingernail well and add diamanté or rhinestones. It can sometimes be a little tricky to place them exactly where you want them without smudging your polish. Using a toothpick gives you more control.

Crazy nails

Paint nails in a pale shade, then, using a fine liquid eyeliner brush, paint on five dots in a deeper colour in the shape of a flower. You can experiment with other shapes too. Try drawing on a star or multicoloured stripes running diagonally across your nail.

Glitter nails

For the ultimate shimmer, press still-wet nails in pale shimmery shades in glitter – or just line the tip with glitter as it dries. Once everything has dried, brush off any loose particles. Then seal with clear varnish.

TOP 5 TIPS FOR FEET

• If you haven't treated your feet for a while, just this once go to a chiropodist and get your feet spoilt for a session. And it has to be a chiropodist – a pedicurist will pretty things up, but they won't do the mega-makeover your forgotten feet probably need right now.

• Once your feet have been treated by the chiropodist, don't wait for them to revert to their previous state before you deal with them again. Your feet will now be at their best, so work on maintaining that perfection.

• Before every bath or shower, spend two or three minutes whisking over your feet with a foot file or pumice to remove dead skin. In a pedicure you do this after you've soaked, but day to day it's better done before your bath as water hydrates the dry skin and you won't always see which areas need to be tackled.

• Give yourself a major pedicure once a month to keep nails under control.

• Treat any unusual problems quickly. While you may not like to think about it, feet do get some nasties on them – and pretty quickly too. So if you get corns, verrucas or fungal infections, sort them out as soon as you notice them. That way they'll go more quickly and nothing evil (like lost toenails) will occur.

MAKE YOUR FOOT TREATMENT

Treat your feet with this homemade foot bath, which will soothe aching limbs and speed up circulation:

Boiling water
Green tea (loose or bags)
Peppermint oil

Fill a bowl full of boiling water. Add five green tea bags – or two scoops of flaked green tea – and three drops of peppermint oil. Wait five minutes and check the water has cooled enough to put your feet in (if it hasn't, add some cool water). Soak your feet for five minutes. Get out, pat them dry and apply foot cream or body lotion.

basic pedicure

If you decide to treat your feet at home, this simple pedicure will remove dead skin and give tired feet a new zest for life.

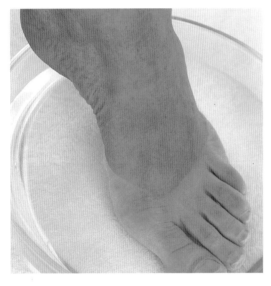

1 Soak your feet in warm water. For a little bit of extra pep add some bicarbonate of soda or a few green tea bags.

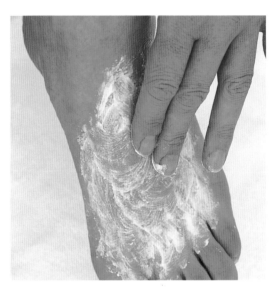

2 Use a salt- or sugar-based body scrub to remove any surface dead skin. Tackle any severe dead skin with a pumice, foot file or electric sander (depending on how bad the problem is), gently removing any thickened, hard or cracked skin.

EASY PEDICURE TIPS

If you think your feet are simply beyond help, indulge in a paraffin wax at a spa. This popular treatment involves painting your feet with warm wax and wrapping them up to help them absorb moisture. The end result is perfectly smooth, soft skin. Get your hands done too for an extra treat.

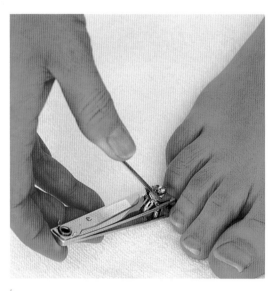 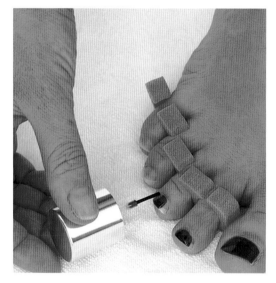

3 Trim your nails. This should be done with clippers only and you should only ever cut straight across. Shaping toenails can lead to ingrowing nails, which can be very painful. Now apply a rich foot cream containing urea to your feet and nails. If you can, pop on some socks, go to bed and paint your nails in the morning. Alternatively, if you're in a rush, after two to three minutes, rub over the nails with a flannel or the edge of a towel. This prepares your nails for painting, but will also help remove any excess cuticles.

4 Paint the toenails. Toe separators will help you avoid polish smudging from one toe to the next. If you don't want to buy toe separators, use tissues pushed between the toes to keep them apart – this is better than cotton wool, which can shed fibres. Paint toenails as you do fingers, with two or three thin coats applied in long strokes. And, as always, don't forget the base coat.

hands and feet Q & A

Let us help you with your most common hand- and footcare questions.

Q: I get dreadful hangnails. How should I deal with them?

A: Hangnails are caused when cuticles grow up the side of the nail. They harden and become separated, creating little 'sticks' at the nail edge. Prevent them by caring regularly for your cuticles. To treat existing ones, however, the most important thing is not to pull them, as this can create painful tears in the skin at the side of the nail which can become infected. Instead, use a cuticle clipper (the only time you should use these) to cut the hangnail as close to the nail as possible. Now apply cuticle remover for five to six minutes to dissolve the rough edge. Finally, apply cuticle oil and push back the rest of the cuticle to prevent the hangnail regrowing.

Q: Why do I have horizontal ridges and white spots on my nails?

A: Both of these are signs of damage to the nail while it was growing. The ridges are disruptions to the pattern of the nail cells, the white spots signs of air under the nail. Some people also find they have vertical ridges on their nails – these are a sign of ageing (caused as cell renewal changes with age). In both cases, the ridges can be smoothed out with a nail buffer. Use this gently (if you feel burning, you're going too hard and asking for more damage) and make sure you moisturize afterwards.

Q: My nails are always soft. Can I eat anything specific to strengthen them?

A: Well, the jelly myth isn't strictly true – there's no proof it actually helps nails. But a generally healthy diet leads to healthy nails. Specific nutrients to look for are calcium (found in dairy products and bony fish), biotin (found in breakfast cereal and wholemeal foods) and vitamin D (found in fortified milk or created in the body through exposure to sunshine), all of which help strengthen nails.

Q: I've always got cracked heels, and so does my mum. Is this hereditary?

A: You can be genetically predisposed to

dry skin anywhere on the body, including the feet, so it could be. However, there may be other causes. If there is a red rash on the soles of the feet or any inflammation or blistering, infection is probably the cause and you need a treatment cream to make things better. Ask a pharmacist, your GP or a chiropodist for advice. If not, the cause is probably your shoes. Slingbacks or mules create a ridge of hard skin where the heel hits the edge of the shoe and are a common cause of heel problems.

Q: I wore bright red nail varnish on my nails for a week and now they're yellow. What can I do?
A: Grab a buffing stick and rub this over the nail. It will remove the top layer of nail cells, which will hopefully remove the yellowing. If this doesn't work, soak the nails in lemon juice for two to three minutes. This will dry them out, so wash your hands well afterwards and apply lots of hand cream.

Q: When do I need to see a chiropodist about feet problems?
A: You can see a chiropodist about any kind of foot problem, no matter how simple. Conditions like dry skin, fungal toenails, corns, calluses and small verrucas can also be initially treated at home using professional products. If they don't improve within two to three weeks or go completely within four to six weeks, see an expert.

Q: I love the way I look in high heels. Is there anything that makes it okay to wear them every day?
A: Technically, no. Very high heels throw the weight forward, putting pressure on the ball of the foot, the hips and the back. However, this doesn't mean you're doomed to flat shoes for ever. These too alter the natural line of the hips and feet and are as bad for you to wear every day as four-inch stilettos. Instead, the ideal heel height is between one and two inches – and obviously the thinner the heel, the higher it will look.

complete beauty book

index

acknowledgements

Author's Acknowledgements:

I'd like to thank the people who helped with this book. Those who provided information include: John Prothero and the excellent team at the Michaeljohn hair salon in Albermarle Street, London, W1; make-up artist Virginia Nichols for her input into the colour section; nutritionist Natalie Savona for answering questions on food and beauty; and Susan Gerrard from the Natural Nail Company who provided information about nail types.

Other thanks go to PR's - Karen Berman, Helen Shelton, and Nomi at Larkspur. Thanks also go to the companies which provided the beautiful products for photography. These were Boots No7, which supplied cosmetic colours; Virgin Cosmetics Company, which provided skincare and bodycare; Michaeljohn's Salon Spa range, which helped with haircare; Eyelure, for nail and eye accessories; and Opal, which provided bodycare accessories.

Publisher's acknowledgements:

With thanks to:
Photographers Trevor Leighton for step-by-step photography and Colin Bowling for still-life; Make-up artists Charlie Duffy at Joy Goodman (using Clarins, Bobbi Brown, Becca and Nars), and Virginia Nichols; Hairstylist Simon Maynard for Lee Stafford (using Fudge).

Picture credits:

Courtesy of Retna Pictures Ltd:
images on pages 10, 12, 14, 16, 18, 20, 22, 78, 82, 86, 90, 98, 101.

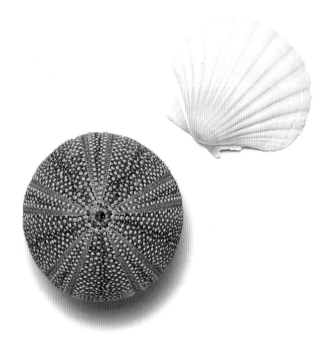